SELECTED POETRY & PROSE OF ILSE AICHINGER

ILSE AICHINGER

SELECTED POETRY & PROSE

Edited & Translated by
ALLEN H. CHAPPEL
With an Introduction by Lawrence L. Langer

LOGBRIDGE-RHODES

Publication of *Selected Poetry & Prose of Ilse Aichinger* was made possible by a grant from the National Endowment for the Arts.

Grateful acknowledgement is also extended to Ilse Aichinger, S. Fischer Verlag, *Dimension, New Orleans Review,* and *Translation.* Specific acknowledgements, along with Library of Congress Cataloging-in-Publication data, may be found on the last printed pages of this book.

Cover/title page illustration is a reproduction of the sculpture "Invictus" by Esther Wertheimer.

This is the first edition.

Printed in the United States of America for:

Logbridge-Rhodes, Inc.
Post Office Box 3254
Durango, Colorado 81301

CONTENTS

INTRODUCTION

Lawrence L. Langer

Ilse Aichinger's prose earns many of the epithets that we apply to much modern literature and art: elusive, obscure, ambiguous. Her vision, though neither derivative nor imitative, since she has a tone and originality distinctively her own, nevertheless rouses numerous reminiscent echoes. Most obvious is Kafka, in whose concrete though insulated atmosphere she seems perfectly at home. The sensitive reader will also discern a bequest from Lewis Carroll, since her serio-comic manipulation of dialogue often resembles some of Alice's lucidly illogical verbal encounters in Wonderland. But the most evident stylistic echo comes from the so-called dramatists of the Absurd, like Beckett and Ionesco, who use language detached from any immediately recognizable social or intellectual mooring to evoke the dilemma of their characters' drifting lives.

Aichinger's lyrical prose evocations are like a grammar of discourse with all questions and certainties omitted, leaving the audience to wonder what remains. "I know, I know" agrees the narrator of one of her pieces, defensively. "Everything wrong. But only in the presentation. The material itself is correct." Of course, this has always been a major challenge to the artist: to find the most dramatic, the most compelling, the most incisive or original or illuminating form for his material. But Aichinger's art questions the validity of presentation itself, and more fundamentally, the power of language to depict the quality of our experience in the twentieth century. She has learned that nothing is what it "is," or how it "is." Then she invents voices obsessed with and possessed by this quandary, and permits them to address an unidentified audience, much like the narrator in Dostoevsky's *Notes from Underground*. We become collaborators, often conspirators in her dilemma, beguiled by her casually playful tone: "You are a listener, one who sounds out others. Only occasionally do you give a shove." Many readers, provoked to exasperation by her failure to say what she means, or *if* she means anything, will give much more than a shove. Some will react uncomfortably to what appears to be *taunting* by certain of her narrative voices. Overwhelmed by a welter of images, unable to fuse them into a unifying insight but equally reluctant to abandon them and return to silence, one of those voices insists on the need to keep talking, to "keep telling her tale," even though the parts never fall into an orderly pattern of lucid ideas. The urgency to communicate despite the lack of cogency in the message is the enigma at the heart of Ilse Aichinger's vision.

Here too she shares frontstage with writers like Beckett and Ionesco, who assume that realistic narrative or drama cannot contend with the bizarre contradictions of twentieth century human experience. She delights in omitting the frame from her pieces, leaving the reader dangling not merely *in medias res*, but in a setting without graspable contours. And this forces us to feel both lost and familiar, consoled and abandoned, since her words are recognizable while the contexts they conjure up are not. In a piece called "Inferior Words," her narrator condones what she calls "assailable expressions" as an adequate option to useless disputes about which word is appropriate to which gesture or experience. Absolute precision is no longer the goal of the writer, who now searches for phrases with which she can "make do." At a loss for a better designation for "life" than the word itself, Aichinger's narrator concludes: "Let's call it *life*, perhaps it deserves nothing better. *Living* is not a special word and *dying* isn't either. Both are assailable, disguising meaning instead of defining it."

The alert reader will detect in these lines a clue to Ilse Aichinger's literary strategy and intentions. Those familiar with her distinguished novel, *Die Grössere Hoffnung (The Greater Hope*, translated into English as *Herod's Children*), a tale of growing up in Vienna during World War II with some "wrong" (Jewish) grandparents and some "right" (non-Jewish) ones (like Ilse Aichinger herself), will have a keener sense of what she means when she speaks of language disguising meaning instead of defining it. During the Third Reich, the designation "wrong" often became a passport to death in Auschwitz (the fate of Aichinger's own grandmother), and the special vocabulary which the Nazis developed, like "resettlement" and "special treatment," would after the War join a long list of "assailable" terms that for a time purged part of the German language of the possibility of exact definition. When disguise rather than definition becomes the *purpose* of one's language, as it did during those years, one inherits a verbal bequest to be regarded as something less than a treasure. Since the experiences of living or dying were so devalued during the deathcamp era, by terror and mass murder, the words representing them suffered an accompanying decline in worth—and to this dubious heritage Aichinger pays homage in her writing. It is as if history had afflicted language with a lingering disease, which through a cunning reversal had then re-infected history, leaving both weakened and objects of suspicion. "I know that the world is worse than its name," says Aichinger's narrator in "Inferior Words," "and that therefore its name too is inferior."

The corruption of language disarms even the wary artist, though to her credit she frankly acknowledges the situation that traps her. "I watch every and each thing assume its speedy and incorrect designation," admits Aichinger's narrator, adding: "recently I've even been joining in. The only difference is: I know what I'm doing." Mistrust of the word becomes a virtue to the conscious fabricator. After World War II, with its revelations about the unholy uses for which language had been recruited in behalf of mass murder, Aichinger confessed her inability to help her countrymen to unlearn the German language. But she *could* help them, she said, "to learn it anew, as a foreigner learns a new language—cautiously, prudently, as one kindles a light in a dark house and continues on one's way." The image reminds us how easy it is to lose our way in the "dark house" of our present reality, led astray by a lazy attention which assumes that words can still be trusted to guide us securely toward the meaning of our lives. When experience contradicts verbal ideas—"the brotherhood of all men" seems particularly appropriate as an example in the context of the Third Reich—then those ideas lose their reference, their durability, and Aichinger's narrator alludes to them with sour disenchantment as her "castoffs," adding: "Oh, well, it doesn't matter what they are called. We have had sufficient proof of that."

The writer then is a phrase-maker relearning her own language, not because she has forgotten it but because history has permanently altered its power of allusion. Without specifying its genesis, Aichinger's narrator in "Inferior Words" invents a striking expression—to "gather the downfall"—but then rejects it because it sounds too good to her: "Too sharp, too precise... a better designation for pure truth than pure truth is." Exactly how many "downfalls" we have gathered in our melancholy century of atrocity need not be recorded here, but to an imagination responsive to those disasters, the task of gathering them might seem as apt a challenge to the truth of our time as words could approach. Unfortunately, the impurity of language frustrates that task.

Members of a civilization bred on the assurance that in the original beginning was the word must now adjust themselves to the shock of recognition that in their *new* beginning is the insufficiency of the word. Aichinger's characters inhabit a world where words have failed the test of precision, where the thing designated has betrayed the role assigned to it by language. Designations deceive until, as Aichinger writes, with a subtle shift to a surprising prefix, everything is left "in its improper perspective" enabling us to see not "better" but merely sufficiently. Like our expectations of life, art has grown more modest. A language of second-best, as she says, is all that is left to us; we have already paid the price for a language of supremacy. And "if that's not inaccurate enough for someone," she adds, playing with unanticipated prefixes once again, "let him quietly try to go further in that direction." Her signposts, if not perfectly lucid, are never simply outrageous; she is determined not to trespass beyond the limits of a carefully restrained ambiguity. The pursuit of controlled inaccuracy is not a willful transgression of clarity, but a recognition of what words cannot do, an assent to the partial collapse of traditional verbal power.

Within these boundaries, Ilse Aichinger carves out her artistic domain. In a brief piece called "My Green Donkey," a narrative voice, shorn of biographical identity or geographical locale, establishes a sharp visual perspective by fixing on a concrete object (the donkey), then invests it with vivid presence without providing any more details about its genesis or purpose than she does about herself. A strange one-way bond develops between the two, to which the reader is silent if puzzled witness, since the donkey seems unaware of the narrator's existence. "In my eyes, thus my donkey," proclaims the narrator, thus furnishing us with a concise formula for Ilse Aichinger's own creative process, which depends so much on visual confirmation. She champions an observant eye rather than a reflective mind, a creator more keen for details than interpretation, a world where the tangible has substance while the speculative evaporates. She refuses to idealize this creature of her imagination, the green donkey: "I don't want to slip back into old mistakes, I wouldn't want to demand too much of it. I want to be satisfied with expecting it or rather with not expecting it." With this reservation in mind, she is prepared to cherish the pleasure of admiring, willing to "learn so little about it that I can also endure its failure to come," ready for the defeat of the imagination even as she celebrates its power to evoke. In other words, the excitement of presence coexists with the prospect of loss—very much the experience of her generation in Europe—and the challenge to author and reader is to relish the one without suppressing response to the eventuality of the other.

Artistic endeavor nourishes the creator as the donkey's arrival sustains her narrator: "its appearance creates air for me to breathe, it alone, its outline, the shades of its green...." The seeds of parable exist in this brief tale, a method for enduring by projecting the content of one's imagination onto the landscape of reality and thus momentarily transfixing the visible world. For a time may come, she says, when she will no longer direct her eyes to the bridge which the donkey crosses, when he will disappear. But until then, imaginative activity enriches reality: "I dream often that it could have a green father and a green mother, a bundle of hay in one of the courtyards over there and in its ears the laughter of the young people who are embracing in the entrance." Rejoice in this present, she suggests at the very end: soon enough sleep will be replaced by dying.

And this is how, I suspect, Ilse Aichinger wishes us to confront her elusive prose, rejoicing in its lyric moments without trying to penetrate to the cavernous recesses of some hidden profundity. In a piece called "Dover," the city on the southern English coast becomes for no particular reason other than the assertion itself the representative of exact equivalence between place and name, designation and thing, incapable of misleading, a city "incorruptible and quiet between snares and imperfections." Nothing inherent in the actual city, neither its history nor its location, merits such celebrity. Rather, the fabricator with words makes it so by stating it and then thrusting its certainty, with variations, on the reader, until the name Dover acquires magical properties possessed by no other place name. "Dover spreads exact inklings," we are told, making it an unaccountable source of reliable and vigorous vison. Unlike other cities, it can "meddle with dispositions without their having a harmful effect upon it." It is somehow immune from social infection, thus can "entreat the places of the world for us with its easy glances." Inexplicably, Dover expresses a need for a center of security in our daily existence, embodying a psychological strength without which that existence could not continue. Dover "will not shove aside failed desperation which is ours," we are told at the very end: "Not Dover."

What can this mean? Dover is first of all simply a word, designating a city. The opening lines of this piece offer a clue to our possible response: "Warld would be better than world. Less useful, less apt. Orth would be better than earth. But this is the way it is now. Normandy is called Normandy and nothing else. The rest also." In the absence of fresh words like "warld" and "orth" in our vocabulary, our only alternative if we would use language to help us see anew is to invent surprising contexts for the old and familiar terms. Hence Dover generates consequences that few would normally identify with it, exemplifying Aichinger's penchant for building her effects on verbal disturbance, reversal of logic, subversion of expected assertion. She compels the reader who does not simply dismiss her as too obscure to listen with a different ear and learn to tolerate and then appreciate the bemusing and often amusing dissociation between experience and what she calls its "lack-lustre designation." The challenge is demanding, but no more so than the one facing the first readers of Henry James's last novels, Faulkner's *The Sound and the Fury*, parts of Joyce's *Ulysses* and most of *Finnegan's Wake*, to say nothing of the perplexed members of the audience at the earliest performances of Beckett's *Waiting for Godot*.

But Dover has associations beyond the word itself, and its conjunction with Normandy in the opening lines of Aichinger's piece could hardly be considered accidental to readers of her generation. The white cliffs of the one signify sanctuary and freedom to those trapped beyond the bloody and dangerous beaches of the other, so that history does loom dimly in the background of Aichinger's evocation here. But its role depends largely on the reader's contribution, since she makes no attempt beyond the naming to attribute meaning to the places. Her strategy forces the reader to reenact the conflict between history and language, as her prose assaults our imagination in multiple waves, old meanings and new verbalizations contending for some kind of satisfactory reconciliation. She is content to remain aloof from the battle, a catalyst whose chief role is to remind us of the value of discovering terms and styles to express our experience that may seem "less useful" and "less apt" than those formerly available. If unassailable expressions could not prevent the debacle that Dover and Normandy still summon up for the informed reader, perhaps we should pay closer attention to the virtue of assailable ones. Insofar as it transcends its original narrow implication and extends the range of verbal possibility, the word "Dover" becomes part of that vocabulary.

Combining the visual with the sensuous, eliminating the abstract, Aichinger's prose, in its fidelity to the exact image and the physical detail, reflects more than a trace of the sensibility of Joyce's Molly Bloom. The memory of her narrator in "The Doll," recalling her childhood and the places she has visited, is filled with spontaneous enthusiasm for things seen and felt. In a passage like the following, odors and sounds and tastes proliferate, invading the reader's senses with the appeal of verbal immediacy:

> This time too I have more like the smell of fish and
> ocean in my clothes and bright frescoes which are still
> preserved from peeling, are still in my mind, and the
> churches of the plains, their rows of birds and shrubs,
> the paths between them which supplicants take, tender
> sighs, blessings, the hands which touch me. Evenings
> were also again in one of the cafés and I got to taste nut-

12

cream, I was promised consolation with the birds up to this very day and then quickly dragged home through markets and the Jews' quarter, we passed also a monastery of St. Dorothy, the consultation hour was over and all were in bed there. We too ourselves went to bed quickly when we reached the room in the hotel.

If life consisted only of the pleasures of remembering, passages such as these would be tonic to Aichinger's aging narrator, and to the weary reader himself. Unfortunately, life also includes the pain of forgetting, the suppression of memories that inspire neither delight nor consoling nostalgia. The voice in "The Doll" is seized by a dual awareness, bright images of joy and melancholy reminders of human insufficiency: "But how far my thoughts lead me, what do I know about monasteries, what do I know at all anyway?" Something has happened, between the past and the present, to cast a shadow of uncertainty over the future. Images continue to speak eloquently throughout the piece, but occasionally a hint of desolation accompanies them: "thus do I lie half sitting, the silk clothes rumpled under the gray cloth, and with open cupboards, the suitcases are gone."

Clusters of images continue to prevail, a hallmark of Aichinger's prose, but clearly there are moments when the artist recognizes even their limitations: now an invitation, now an obstacle to despair. In her gloomy moments, their power wanes for her: "Only these chests, empty drawers, the fragrance of lavender and I'll forget to whom I belong, forget forgetting and forgetting will forget me." And if this were a permanent condition, the narrator's voice would gradually fade and be silenced. Fortunately, it is not, though this is a source of wonder rather than support for the now tired narrator: "Remarkable that the mountain ranges still appear to me and caravans over the passes and how the large animals turn their heads toward the old chapels." Concrete visual affirmations of reality flood her imagination as summoners to creative possibility. But the weary rememberer, in the closing line of her narrative, seems more responsive to beckoning death: "And I want only to meet up with the waving hands in front of the red stone in my sleep." Such indirect narration is a constant challenge to the reader, who must grow accustomed to the habit of "hearing visually," then translating those image-sounds into legitimate meaning. Or illegitimate meaning, as Aichinger perhaps would prefer, since a word like "legitimate" is one of those old unassailable expressions that has been corrupted by the seducers of history and familiarity.

"Hearing visually" is a precise description of the challenge presented by one of Aichinger's longest pieces, the radio play

(Hörspiel) "The Jouet Sisters" (which is also included in this collection in a shorter narrative version). It documents the persuasive power of language to invent realities that compel our belief despite our foreknowledge of their non-existence. We are enticed into a milieu that slowly displaces our own with its vague but tantalizing allusions to circumstances and persons existing only within the creative vision of the sister Rosalie, who then imposes the content of this vision on the other two, now reluctant, now hostile sisters — Anna and Josepha. For example, an exasperated Josepha at one moment protests to Rosalie: "I prefer everything without your fabrications. The way it is. Even the bubonic plague." The voice of the usual speaks here, preferring familiar evils to ills (or pleasures) it knows not of, a voice dismayed and frightened by detours of the imagination that chart seemingly arid and uninhabited landscapes, a voice fatal to art. But Rosalie pursues the task of fabrication, knowing that for her it is the sole remaining weapon for holding off a reality that threatens to consume her spirit.

"The Jouet Sisters" is a play with the exposition missing, so that the audience is required to furnish one—or to admit that "exposition" is one of those ancient expectations which modern experience has purged of its former substance. Talk of "fabrication" dominates the verbal action, until we are forced to reconsider the fine line separating actual from invented reality and to ask which plays a more influential role in our lives. The sisters are by definition, as Josepha says, "named and unnamed conversation partners," gifted with speech but deprived of logical sequences of expression—as men and women may be gifted with the capacity for virtue but deprived of a sustaining context for its logical expression by a society committed to violence. If speech is divorced from act, vision from consequence, are our lives then merely the roles we adopt in a drama without larger reference, without "exposition," as it were, an existence shorn of meaningful human communion? One of the refrains repeated near the end of "The Jouet Sisters" is "COME BACK," confirming a loss or absence though we are never sure who or what is summoned. We are left instead with a sense of being bereft, but without the accompanying anxiety one has learned to expect from analogous writers like Kafka and Beckett. Uncertainty prevails in Aichinger's work as in theirs, but we are never overwhelmed by the looming possibility of despair, perhaps because she still finds some lingering cause for hope in her private sanctuary of language.

If her usage is eccentric (and what original art is not?), her resolution is straightforward and courageous. Like Rosalie in

14

"The Jouet Sisters," Aichinger is untroubled by the embarrassment her "fabricating" may bring upon those who cherish the security of the conventional. What will they think, asks sister Anna, of someone like you who is determined to "register us with the reputation of peculiarity"? Aichinger, like her persona Rosalie, would view this as a compliment, and would repeat, as had Rosalie earlier: "Listen, stop, I shall fabricate new words for you...." The constant search for new sources of verbal vitality and felicity, combined with the steady erosion of old norms and forms by fresh imaginative vision, are the stimulants of Ilse Aichinger's art. New words lead to new worlds, in the realm of the imagination if not yet within the more limited boundaries of actual experience. Readers will have to decide for themselves whether to retreat to the safety of the familiar or to advance into the insecurity of a dislocated prose. But those venturing onto this terrain, Ilse Aichinger's Otherland, will meet verbal surprises at every turning which more than repay the efforts of their precarious journey.

POEMS

ALTER BLICK

Ich habe mich gewöhnt an dieses Fenster
und dass der Schnee durch meine Augen fällt,
aber wer ist den Verlorenen nachgegangen
durch das offene Gartentor,
wer besiegelte, was da war,
die Regentonne
und den Mond als Mond,
alle gefrorenen Gräser?
Wer schaukelte vor dem Morgen,
dass die Stricke krachten,
wer legt die Wachshand auf das Küchenfenster,
liess sich im Weissen nieder
und nahm mich selber auf?

GLIMPSE FROM THE PAST

I've gotten used to this window
and to the snow falling through my eyes,
but who has followed the lost ones
through the open garden gate,
who left his seal upon what was there,
the rain barrel
and the moon as moon,
every frozen blade of grass?
Who rocked before dawn,
and made the ropes crack,
who lays his wax hand on the kitchen window,
lay down in whiteness
and accepted me myself?

ZEITLICHER RAT

Zum ersten
musst du glauben,
dass es Tag wird,
wenn die Sonne steigt.
Wenn du es aber nicht glaubst,
sage ja.
Zum zweiten
musst du glauben
und mit allen deinen Kräften,
dass es Nacht wird,
wenn der Mond aufgeht.
Wenn du es aber nicht glaubst,
sage ja
oder nicke willfährig mit dem Kopf,
das nehmen sie auch.

TEMPORAL ADVICE

First
you must believe
that day will come,
when the sun rises.
But if you don't believe it,
say yes.
Second
you must believe
and with all your strength,
that night will come,
when the moon rises.
But if you don't believe it,
say yes
or nod your head obligingly,
they accept that too.

MÖGLICHKEITEN

Dass ich,
wenn ich mit meiner linken Schulter
den Spiegelschrank streife,
einem Meineidigen helfe
wie einem, der stirbt,
dass ein anderer,
einer in der Touraine,
einer im Niedergang,
wenn ich das Licht bei mir ausdrehe,
den nächsten Schritt wieder sieht,
dass ein dritter,
wenn ich zwischen den kranken Stämmen bei uns
schlafen gehe,
zwischen ganz anderen
und gesunden Stämmen,
aber mit einem leichten, kräftigen Seil
bei der Hand,
hinaus auf die Wiesen geht.

POSSIBILITIES

That I
when I brush against the wardrobe
with my left shoulder,
am aiding a perjurer
like one who is dying,
that another,
one in Touraine,
one in downfall,
when I turn out the light in my room,
sees again the next step,
that a third,
when I go to sleep
between the diseased tree trunks at home,
goes out onto the meadow
between quite different
and healthy trunks
but with a light, powerful rope at hand.

RESTLOS

Die Jungen mit den Totenscheinen
sind verschwunden.
Sie sind auf den gewesenen Pferden
rasch aus den Basaren geritten.
Sie sind fort.

Uns bleibt zu bedenken:
die List der Saurier
und wie sie kleiner wurden
bis zu unserem Masse,
die Spuren der Verwerfung
und ihr blankes Ende,
Hilfe und Hinweis
und ihr Untergang.

COMPLETELY

The boys with the death certificates
have disappeared.
They rode on has-been horses
quickly out of the bazaars.
They are gone.

There remains for us to consider:
the cunning of the saurians
and how they grew smaller
down to our dimension,
traces of rejection
and their total expiration,
help and hint
and their decline.

NEUER BUND

Die Sonne will vor mir
in meinen Frieden,
springt, drängt, bewegt sich läppisch,
wartet mich nicht ab.
Und darum geh ich fort
aus diesem Frieden,
aus diesem lieben Frieden
in den Schatten
zu meinen lieben Schweinen,
die allein grimmig und gelassen genug
nach dem Gebote
und nach den Geboten
in unserem stumpfen Wasser
zu ersticken wissen,
die keine Sonne einholt
und verdirbt,
die obenauf erst nach dem Ende bleiben.
Meine Könige.

NEW ALLIANCE

The sun wants to move before me
into my tranquility,
jumps, pushes, moves childishly,
doesn't wait for me.
And for that reason
I'm leaving this tranquility,
this lovely tranquility
in the shade
to go to my lovely swine,
who alone know how
to be suffocated
violently and calmly enough
in our dull water,
according to the command
and according to the commandments
swine which no sun overtakes
and destroys,
which remain uppermost only after the end.
My kings.

IN WELCHEN NAMEN

Der Name Alissa,
der Name Inverness,
wann und
von welchen Wüstenrändern
hergetragen,
durch welche Orden,
Mönchsorden, Schwesternorden,
längs oder quer
und wohin, wohin nicht,
wie haltbar,
wie versch wenderisch
mit Mauerringen,
unter Wintersonnen
in aufgerissene Gräben,
Wälle, Wiegen
mit Feuern, Ringellocken,
ach Namen, Namen,
wenigstens auf euch beide
bin ich ungetauft
und bin nicht schuld.

IN WHICH NAMES

The name Alissa,
the name Inverness,
when and
dragged up
from what edges of desolation,
through which orders
monastic, conventual orders
lengthwise or diagonal
and whence, whence not,
how durable,
how wasteful
with wall rings,
under winter suns
into opened ditches,
embankments, cradles
with fires, ringlets,
oh names,names,
at least with
neither of you two am I christened
and bear no guilt.

TEIL DER FRAGE

Hoch auf dem Platze steht das Wasser,
die Luft steigt noch in Blasen,
doch was sie singen,
dringt nicht mehr zu mir.
Die Fische kreisen um die Kirchentüren,
wer gibt mir Antwort:
Soll ich in den Berg
oder ins Haus mit denen,
die mich lieben,
und den weiten Blick,
das Knirschen aller Schritte
noch einmal?
Wie schwarz mein Land wird,
nur tief unten krümmt sich
grün die Zeit.

PART OF THE QUESTION

High up on the square stands the water,
the air still rises in bubbles,
but what they are singing
no longer reaches me.
The fish circle around the church doors,
who'll answer me:
Should I go into the mountain
or into the house with those
who love me,
and the distant view,
the grating of every footstep
once more?
How black my country becomes,
only deep down does
time wriggle green.

SCHNEELEUTE

Ich mische mich nicht leicht
unter die Fremden aus Schnee
mit Kohlen, Rüben, Hölzern,
ich rühre sie nicht an,
solang sie heiter prangen,
manche mit mehr Gesichtern
als mit einem.
Wenn dann die Kohlen
und die Rüben fallen,
Knöpfe, Knopfleisten,
die roten Lippenbänder,
seh ich es steif mit an
und ohne Laut,
ich eile nicht zu Hilfe.
Vielleicht sprechen sie
das Mailändische
schöner als ich,
es soll nicht ans Licht kommen.
Und darum Stille,
bis dieses Licht sie leicht
genommen hat
mit allem, was sich da
zwischen mailändisch
und mailändisch verbirgt,
dann auch mit mir.

SNOW PEOPLE

I don't mix easily
with strangers made of snow
with coal, turnips, sticks of wood,
I do not touch them,
as long as they glisten cheerfully,
some with more faces
than one.
Then when the coals
and the turnips fall,
buttons, button beading
the red lip-bands,
I watch it stiffly
and without a sound,
I do not rush to help.
Maybe they speak
Milanese better than I,
that is not to come to light.
And therefore stillness,
until this light has
taken them
with everything that
is hidden there between
Milanese and Milanese
then also including me.

ZUSPRUCH AN EINEN MANN, DER DREIUNDZWANZIG JAHRE IM BETT BLIEB UND DANN AUFSTAND

Die Sekunden
am Bettrand entlang
freue dich,
so freu dich doch,
sage ich dir,
im Namen der Stadt
Newcastle upon Tyne,
der Schafschur,
die du so beherzt
mit ansahst,
der neuen Zucht,
die dich den Schweinen
überlegen macht,
noch überlegener,
der hübschen Pfiffe
aus Schottland,
hin und her,
steh nicht versteint
im Morgen,
freue dich.

WORDS ADDRESSED TO A MAN WHO REMAINED IN BED
TWENTY-THREE YEARS AND THEN GOT UP

Rejoice
the seconds
along the bed's edge,
thus do rejoice,
I say to you,
in the name of the city
Newcastle upon Tyne,
of sheep shearing,
during which you watched
so valiantly,
of the new breed
which makes you
superior to the pigs,
even more superior,
of the pretty whistles
from Scotland,
back and forth,
do not stand petrified
in the morning,
rejoice.

MEINER GROSSMUTTER

Die Doppeltüren
in den Modenapark,
die Frage
nach dem Ursprung,
nach den Religionen,
die Salesiandergasse,
die Frau Major Schultz,
die Excellenz Zwitkowitsch,
das Erschrecken,
die Demut,
die Abhängigkeit,
das Fräulein Belmont,
die Zuflucht,
der fremde Flur,
das Tor,
das aufspringt,
der tolle Hund,
erschrick nicht,
er ist weiss,
noch klein
und läuft vorbei.

TO MY GRANDMOTHER

The double-doors
into Modena park,
the question
about origin,
about religions,
Salesiander Street,
wife of Major Schultz,
wife of Excellency Zwitkowitsch,
terror,
humility,
dependence,
Miss Belmont,
flight,
the strange entrance hall,
the gate,
which springs open,
the mad dog,
don't be afraid,
it is white,
still small
and runs past.

EINUNDDREISSIG

Ich lasse mich gerne gehen
und nehm die dreissig Silberlinge mit,
wenn einer sie mir gibt,
mit um den Hals,
sodass wir schaukeln können,
wir einunddreissig
und dass ich sie noch klirren höre
in ihrem Hanfsack
bis aus der Welt.
Dass ich, wenn mir die Zunge steif wird,
doch noch mit meinen blanken Ohren
die Stimme mitbekomme,
die euch gebietet:
Beginnt noch einmal!
Dass ich dann lustig bin.

THIRTY-ONE

I let myself walk with pleasure
and take the thirty pieces of silver along,
if someone gives them to me,
to go around my neck,
so we can teeter-totter
we thirty-one
and so that I hear them jingle still
in their hemp-sack
till gone from the world.
So that I, when my tongue grows stiff,
with my bare ears,
still catch the voice
which bids you:
Begin again!
So that I am happy then.

SELBSTGEBAUT

Ich will meine Dörfer
ohne Worte lassen
und nur den Schnee
durchschwingen
und offen gegen die Zäune.
Von der Höhe meiner Speicher
will ich die Jaguare betrachten,
die Wölfe pfeifen hören.
Die Sonne sprang hier fort,
aber den Kindern
wird bei ihrer Ernte
von Löwenzähnen geholfen,
Platz für den König!

SELF-BUILT

I wish to leave
my villages without words
and to swing arms and legs
only through the snow
openly against the fences.
From the height of my silos
I wish to observe the jaguars,
to hear the wolves screeching.
The sun jumped away here,
but the children
at their harvest
will be helped by dandelions,
Seat for the king!

DREIZEHN JAHRE

Das Laubhüttenfest ist weit,
der Glanz der Kastanien,
aufgereiht am Fenster des Gartenhauses.
Und noch im Raum
die Kerze,
die Religionen der Welt.

Der Wüstenstaub unter dem Fahrradschlauch.
Nach diesem Mittag
kommt die Dämmerung schneller.
Die Gefährten
und ein grünes Grab,
Rajissa.

Wir kommen abends wieder,
wir kommen nimmermehr.

THIRTEEN YEARS

The Feast of Tabernacles is far away,
the radiance of chestnuts,
lined up at the window of the summer-house.
And still in the room
the candle,
the religions of the world.

The desert dust under the bicycle tube.
After this noon
the twilight comes quicker.
The fellow travellers
and a green grave,
Rajissa.

We'll return evenings,
we'll come nevermore.

ABGEZÄHLT

Der Tag, an dem du
ohne Schuhe ins Eis kamst,
der Tag, an dem
die beiden Kälber
zum Schlachten getrieben wurden,
der Tag, an dem ich
mir das linke Auge durchschoss,
aber nicht mehr,
der Tag, an dem
in der Fleischerzeitung stand,
das Leben geht weiter,
der Tag, an dem es weiterging.

ENUMERATION

The day on which you
came into the ice without shoes,
the day on which
the two calves
were driven to slaughter,
the day on which I
pierced my left eye,
but no longer,
the day on which
the butcher's newspaper read,
life goes on,
the day on which it continued.

BRIEFWECHSEL

Wenn die Post nachts käme
und der Mond
schöbe die Kränkungen
unter die Tür:
Sie erschienen wie Engel
in ihren weissen Gewändern
und stünden still im Flur.

CORRESPONDENCE

If the mail came at night
and the moon
shoved insults
under the door:
They would seem like angels
in their white garments
and would stand quietly in the vestibule.

MARIANNE

Es tröstet mich,
dass in den goldenen Nächten
ein Kind schläft.
Dass sein Atem neben der Schmiede geht
und seine Sonne
schon früh
mit Hahn und Hennen
über das nasse Gras steigt.

MARIANNE

It consoles me
that a child sleeps
in golden nights.
That its breath goes next to the smithy
and its sun
already early
with rooster and hens
rises above the damp grass.

BREITBRUNN

Es neigen sich
die Tage der Kindheit
den späten Tagen zu.
Und fragst du nach der Heimat,
so sagen alle, die blieben:
Das Gras ist gewachsen.
Aber nichts davon,
dass die gewundenen Wege
die Hügel hinab
aufstanden und seufzten.
Ehe sie sterben,
ziehen die Pfarrer
in andere Dörfer.

BREITBRUNN

The days of childhood
are bending down
to latter days.
And if you ask about home
then all say, who remained:
The grass has grown.
But nothing about the fact
that the twisted paths
down the hill
stood up and sighed.
Before they die
the pastors move
to other villages.

UNSERE FRAU

Unsere Frau
gehört zum Klageverein,
sie fährt mit dem Rad zur Scheune,
beklagt die Lebenden.
Die Butterblumen leuchten ihr, der Bach,
wenn sie die Augen schliesst,
fliegt rot der Steinbruch vorbei.

OUR WOMAN

Our woman
belongs to the complaint union
she rides her bicycle to the barn
deplores the living.
The buttercups illumine her,
                the brook,
when she closes her eyes
the quarry flies past red.

CHINESISCHER ABSCHIED

Wir legen uns heute nieder,
doppelt nieder,
wer unds wecken will,
möge es sanft tun,
er möge seine Stimme schonen
und auch sein Herz,
denn beide sind kostbar.

CHINESE FAREWELL

Today we lie down,
doubled down,
he who wishes to wake us,
may he do it softly,
let him spare his voice
and also his heart,
for both are precious.

WIDMUNG

Ich schreibe euch keine Briefe,
aber es wäre mir leicht, mit euch zu
        sterben.
Wir liessen uns sacht die Monde hinunter
und läge die erste Rast noch bei den
        wollenen Herzen,
die zweite fände uns schon mit Wölfen
        und Himbeergrün
und dem nichts lindernden Feuer, die
        dritte, da wär ich
durch das fallende dünne Gewölk mit
        seinen spärlichen Moosen
und das arme Gewimmel der Sterne, das
        wir so leicht überschritten,
in eurem Himmel bei euch.

DEDICATION

I write you no letters,
but it would be easy for me
         to die with you.
We would let ourselves gently down the moons
and if the first resting place were still
         with woollen hearts,
the second would find us already
         with wolves and raspberry green
and with the fire alleviating nothing,
         the third, there I would be
through the thin falling cloud mass
         with its scanty mosses
and the meagre throng of stars that
         we would so easily step over,
in your heaven with you.

TAGSÜBER

Ein ruhiger Junitag
bricht mir die Knochen,
verkehrt mich,
schleudert mich ans Tor,
hängt mir die Nägel an,
die mit den Farben
gelb, weiss und silberweiss,
verfehlt mich nicht,
mit keinem,
lässt nur die Narrenmütze fort,
mein Lieblingsstück,
würgt mich
mit seinen frischen Schlingen
solang bis ich noch atme.
Bleib, lieber Tag.

DURING THE DAY

A peaceful June day
breaks my bones,
turns me around,
hurls me at the gate,
catches on my nails,
those with colors
yellow, white and silver-white,
doesn't mistake me
for anyone else,
only leaves out the fool's cap,
my favorite thing,
chokes me
with its green tendrils
as long as I still breathe.
Remain, beloved day.

GËBIRGSRAND

Denn was täte ich,
wenn die Jäger nicht wären, meine Träume,
die am Morgen
auf der Rückseite der Gebirge
niedersteigen, im Schatten.

MOUNTAIN CREST

For what would I do,
if there weren't the hunters, my dreams,
which in the morning
climb down the back side of the mountains,
in the shade.

PROSE & DIALOGUES

INFERIOR WORDS

I now no longer use better words. *The rain which pounds against the windows*. Formerly something quite different would have occurred to me. Now this is sufficient. *The rain which pounds against the windows*. That's adequate. Anyway, I just had another different expression on the tip of my tongue, it was not only better, it was more precise, but I forgot it, while the rain was pounding against the windows or was doing that which I was in the process of forgetting. I'm not very curious what will occur to me during the next rain, be it a kind of shower or a heavy downpour, but I presume that a turn of phrase for all kinds of rain will be adequate. I won't worry whether one can say *pound* when it only lightly touches the window panes, whether that isn't then an overstatement. Or whether it is an understatement when it is about to break in the window panes. I'll leave it at that, I'll stick to *pound*, others can worry about the rest.

Dragging along downfall in front of one, that occurred to me too, it is certainly more assailable than the pounding rain, for one drags nothing in front of himself, one pushes it or kicks it, carts, for example, or wheelchairs, while one drags along other things like potato sacks, other things, but by no means downfalls, they are promoted some other way. I know that, and already the better phrase was again just on the tip of my tongue, but only to slip my mind. I'll not mourn its loss. *Dragging along downfall in front of one* or better *downfalls*, I'll not insist on one or the other, but I'll stick to the latter. Whether one can say, *I decide on it* is questionable. Up to now usage hasn't allowed one to use *decision* in those instances when there is a question of only one possibility. One could discuss it, but I am fed up with these discussions—they are usually held in taxis on the way out of town—and I make do with my assailable expressions.

Naturally I'll not be able to sell them, but I feel sorry for them just as I feel sorry for prompters and opera glass manufacturers. I begin to acquire a weakness for the second and third best expression in front of which the good hides quite cleverly, and is seen often by the public even if only when taking the fourth best into consideration. One can't take exception to that, the public expects that, the good has no choice. Or has it? Could it not hide from the public and turn up in those expressions which are possible but weaker? One has to wait and see. There are enough adequate devices—complicated to learn thoroughly—and if I lean heavily on those which are inadequate, that's my affair.

I have become careful also in the formation of correlations. I don't say, *while the rain pounds against the windows, we drag downfalls along in front of us,* but I say, *the rain which pounds against the windows* and *dragging downfalls along in front of one* and so forth. No one can demand that I produce correlations as long as they are avoidable. I am not indiscriminate as life is, a better designation for which has also just escaped me. Let's call it *life,* perhaps it deserves nothing better. *Living* is not a special word and *dying* isn't either. Both are assailable, disguising meaning instead of defining it. Perhaps I know why. Defining borders on undermining and exposes one to the grip of dreams. But I must not know that. I can make do. Indeed I can easily make do. I can stick with it. Surely I could say *living* to myself so often that I would get sick of it and would see myself compelled to go to another designation. And *dying* even more often. But I don't do it. I restrict myself and make observations, with that I am sufficiently occupied. I also listen, but that has certain dangers. Doing that, ideas can easily occur to one. Not long ago it was said, *gather the downfall,* it sounded like a command. I wouldn't like that. If it were a request, then one could think it over, but commands frighten me. For that reason also I changed to second best. The best is commanded. Therefore, I don't let myself be frightened anymore. I have had enough of that. And I have had more than enough of my ideas which are not mine at all because they formally meant something different. They can be called *my castoffs* but not *my ideas.* Oh, well, it doesn't matter what they are called. We have had sufficient proof of that. The least best expressions can defend themselves. They come into the world and are immediately surrounded by everything that is inadequate to surround them. Before they can turn their heads, meanings inspired by their own names are attributed to them which are inappropriate. They are already easily discernible in lullabyes. Later that process becomes more massive. And I? I could defend myself. I could easily keep track of the best instead of next-best, but I don't do it. I don't want to be obvious, I like rather to blend in unobtrusively. I observe. I watch every and each thing assume its speedy and incorrect designation, recently I've been joining in. The only difference is: I know what I'm doing. I know that the world is worse than its name and that therefore its name too is inferior.

66

Gather the downfall—that sounds too good to me. Too sharp, too precise, too much like bird calls late at night, a better designation for pure truth than pure truth is. I could attract attention with that, could be lifted from my position in the ranks of name-givers which has been acquired with time and effort, and lose my observation post. No, I'll give that up. I'll remain with my rain which pounds against the windows, in the area of suitable cock-and-bull stories—and if there are to be downfalls, then such ones that one drags along in front of himself. The last is almost too precise, perhaps one should leave downfalls out of the picture altogether. They are too close to that for which they stand, quiet decoy birds that circle around the norm. The norm is good, it is in any case imprecise enough, the norm and the rain, which pounds, all first and last names, the process is endless and one remains the quiet observer, that one would like to be, by chance observed from one direction or the other, while one leaves his fists in his pockets and leaves the downfalls to themselves, leaves them out, leaves them be, that is good. Leaves them be is again too well expressed, ridiculously well expressed, no, leave out the downfalls, they attract undesired precision and do not occur in any lullabye.

The rain which pounds against the windows, there we have it again, we'll leave it, it leaves everything in its improper perspective, we'll stay with that, in order that *we* remains we, in order that everything remains what it is not, from the weather to the angels.

In this way one can live and in this way one can die, and if that is not inaccurate enough for someone, let him quietly try to go further in this direction. For him there are no limits.

THE DOLL

To bed with clothes and no one who might have warmed my waxen face, traces of the morning sweeping through the curtains, eyes half open. There were always such hours or half hours, foreign voices and quite strange walls spotted by the sun.

Was I not just yesterday carried through the city, in thin arms, covered with lace and a hat trimmed with lace on my head? We even went past palaces, courts consisting of columns, the weeds with their light heads were sprouting out of the halls, then cafés, columns again and my girlfriends in the arms of the others who were whispering of forgotten revolutions, and I got to taste raspberry water from a glass and a piece of dry cake, and was consoled: In the evening you'll have a tasty little bird, my love!

And it was already continuing in the churches where the coolness fell down upon us from floorboards of the pulpit, the various sounds of steps on wood and stone, I was sitting in dark benches my sight directed straight ahead not diverted by the rosy lights through the windows. And then into cheese shops, with artificial light, and sitting on a keg, and a little fan that changed the air for me, the laughter of the saleslady. I was manoeuvered carefully over bridges in the sunset and held over ponds, over man-made bodies of water which ran around grassy plots, past old mews, indeed I found myself in the middle of a conversation about the question of old mews, of their reconstruction or other use and no one hid anything from me, deep and high voices about this question were given over to me and crossed at my head thoughtlessly. And I tottered on off under the evening skies and was admired or consoled with wine, quietened with the reflection of the lights on the double windows. Thus peacefully I was able to hear the gates bang open and shut, and to hear the songbirds grow silent and was laid in the middle of it on my arms and cradled like someone after a grave sorrow or like a very small child: and caressed with tears when I was once on the verge of falling in the water but didn't. And I was only set up straight when others like me were approaching, the veil was lightly drawn back from my hat and my round arms where they came out of the lace were stroked, my face covered with kisses when the others like me were gone, so that it seemed to me sometimes as if blood entered my cheeks. And still a long time before we were home, that is before we saw the inn before us again, I was sung to sleep. With the most beautiful songs, a Spanish one supposedly among them.

I know that they almost hadn't taken me along on this as also on many other of our trips but after long imploring entreaties (not mine) I was finally after all quickly fetched from my cradle, my clothes and other necessary things were quickly stowed away in the white and green basket, then I was tottering down the stairs, between this gust of voices before a happy trip, of envy and good disposition in the stairway and the soft breeze under the gateway moved my hair, before a silk kerchief was tied around my hat.

Train, auto or carriage, I slept a lot and the places of arrival divided themselves up for me with their morning and evening lights or doves and with the great amount of stone in the squares of arrival. And people who put themselves at our service, but I was never given over to other arms.

I have a slight recollection that once on a journey to the mountains even daughters of a notary took pleasure in me, I still have in my ears their shouts through the reddish stone, and I was held up backwards to answer their greeting, then they waved and waved to me, their fresh arms moved against the snow which still lay there, and the youngest of them cried before they returned to the houses and wooden terraces, a little bit later she is said to have come further south for instruction, precisely she. But this trip was only one of many, we usually leave the mountains quickly behind unless we were visiting distant relatives.

This time too I have more like the smell of fish and ocean in my clothes and bright frescoes which are still preserved from peeling, are still in my mind, and the churches of the plains, their rows of birds and shrubs, the paths between them which supplicants take, tender sighs, blessings, the hands which touch me. Evenings we were also again in one of the cafés and I got to taste nut-cream, I was promised consolation with the birds up to this very day and then quickly dragged home through markets and the Jews' quarter, we passed also a monastery of St. Dorothy, the consultation hour was over and all were in bed there. We too ourselves went to bed quickly when we reached the room in the hotel.

And now no one is here any more and I cannot turn around by myself to see whether hat and shawl are still hanging on the bed knob. I kept thinking we would later attend together one of those schools where one spends free hours under acacias or wild chestnuts, that I would be held in arms when jumping rope begins, and would be put to rest in wooden monastery beds like some fellow-travelling girlfriends, and that past revolutions would continue to lull me to rest, thus we would grow towards the old lights even if I didn't change my size.

But thus do I lie half sitting, the silk clothes rumpled up under the gray cloth, and with open cupboards, the suitcases are gone.

I think over now whether the monastery of this saint is to blame for everything. Wasn't I supposed to be taken in there? Were my arms too rosy perhaps for the woman gatekeeper, my feet too tender and the expression of my eyes under the golden blond lashes about which I can do nothing, too calm? Or did it tell too much about birds and stairways, about mews and cake, about the raspberry waters which I had sipped? And even about those that I only saw shimmering in the glass, about the gleaming fronts of palaces, about the market stands under the red hurricane lamps past which I was only carried? Was my coat too artfully tied up for her, my veil too delicately filegreed? And did I think it was unjust or not?

But how far my thoughts lead me, what do I know about monasteries, what do I know at all anyway? Wouldn't there be easier and more weighty reasons in superabundance and directions as many as God created which sailors imputed to the compass cards in the stony courts of castles in order to leave them alone in the sun? Would there not be enough low walls to jump over away from me, higher ones to climb over silently? Sons and brothers or just hasty departures for the sake of which I could be forgotten? Whatever gave me the idea I was left in the lurch for my own sake, that one had, as it were, gone from me to me and was looking for me, myself, now everywhere that I am not? And knew then nevertheless a place in which I could not be. What brought me to this woman gatekeeper with her youthfulness and her stern face which I never saw? With the garland of songs around her head and shoulders?

How many more solemn vows do I need now, who is to waken me, who is to fetch me again? For I do not lie in sleep, I am as warm as I am cold, I am alienated from pains, dangers, songs of the saints. No gatekeeper's room will accept me and there will be no conversation about whether I am allowed or not, I shall not perceive the shadows of the clocktowers over the rough curtains blindly in the morning either, in order to be raised up soon, no, none of that. It seems to me now that only the directions which lead behind me are open with their air currents, their unknown, their unenticing colors. With gardens bursting into bloom about which I would like to know so little. I can end no longer now, no gutters in the early light, no ditch over which the alder trees stand watch, and the roaring cars alongside, nothing will hide me, no marsh which preserves my bright feet. Only these chests, empty drawers, the fragrance of lavender and I'll forget to whom I belong, forget forgetting and forgetting will forget me. From then on whoever would like me will be able to fetch me, girl or market lady or the nurse who patches my lace and keeps it from falling apart. A St. George, an abandoned stable and bean pods, I don't want to dream much any more. They can decorate the angels' heads with my curls, the green satin coats with my lace, but with me myself? Wax and strings. And the notary's daughters and the hours for consultation in the monasteries of the saints are not even far away any more.

Remarkable that the mountain ranges still appear to me and caravans over the passes and how the large animals turn their heads towards the old chapels. And I want only to meet up with the waving hands in front of the red stone in my sleep.

FIVE PROPOSALS

I propose a lady in a gray dress with a red collar on it. Nothing is to be mixed. Not the collar and not the dress either. Nothing is to be asserted which is not asserted. Birdlike but not forced, that distinguishes her best. She must be capable of climbing stairs up and down, of stopping, of turning around, many skills. Also of being turned back and of being covered with varnish. The corners are often not measured out, no one is found to be prepared. I am no tool, the lady is accustomed to say. That doesn't make her appearance any easier. Worries of being overtaken by winter are foreign to her. She says arrogantly, I have enough bast. Now it's the business of society to be amazed. Step for step, always with sleep, it is good this way. Objections enough present themselves. She walks stiff-legged, she has no feet, therefore the bast. Her hair is also not in order. Yarn, wool, thread, unwound, worked up, unravelled again, there is nothing it could be compared to. That is always a misfortune. And the color fluctuates with thunderstorms. Often she meets Emperor Ferdinand outside the place. Always to the north, who knows how she gets there? One sees: nothing about her is simple except the dress and perhaps the feet. I therefore ask for indulgence with the red collar. I proposed it just as I proposed her. But I hear voices of opposition, more powerful proposals, more pronounced views. To be misunderstood so quickly comes like homage. One misunderstands me, I wouldn't want to insist. I was just thinking.

With the Emperor Ferdinand it is different. He is wearing bright blue, crosses the street quickly always obliquely and admires details even in far advanced positions. He gives away gateways and wells as places of rendezvous. That is stupid, for someone or other is always behind him, be it the French, be it the Americans of the northwest. But he spends the night in damp rooms, that keeps him young and he cannot be destroyed by the fleeing earth. He says he prefers to use paths upwards rather than downwards. Which paths? Mountain paths, are there others? Of course, level ones, those with the dried ranunculi left and right. Oh, those. He doesn't use those at all. Yet once he did but as a private person. Purely private. Can he swear to that? That he can. He's just hard to catch up with. Before one suspects, one is already ahead of him and then he is not to be found, is conversing with farmers in the bushes about the wood condition and latifundia, while one hurries panting through mountain peaks far ahead. He takes wood conditions seriously, that makes him difficult. He is not a simple emperor, he is often ahead of us. Too quick for imperial concepts and in speed too thoughtful. Many will confirm that. We'll drop him.

An epic in the form of roses: I mean roses mixed among the verses. That would have to be authenticated, the roses clearly to be seen too. People will restrain themselves from that otherwise. Not to be depended on, they'll say, and will write it in their grievances. Or: When I was hurrying past your show windows recently there was no rose in the center. But doesn't the ground rule provide for a lateral exhibition, one in the shadow, and prescribe stronger eyes to those hurrying past? We must follow that one, we must call upon the opticians. Why? Who depends on such subterfuges? Then wouldn't it also be possible to use staves wrapped in green instead of green ones? That's it, and subterfuges for losers are what's best in the ground rule. But then would it also be possible to fasten roses with varnish instead of with the help of vegetation? That's it, that's it. And let's be honest, how often was vegetation conceived of as a nail in cases of necessity? A beautiful epic. Did I say that? I said: shadows and sides are good enough for that if not specifically invented for that. And let's assume, someone has too many lenses or herbs in the store and can't get rid of them, doesn't want to get rid of them either, he has sympathy. What is left for him but to seek out the edges with careful steps? And what happens finally with the roses? They are greeted. Vegetation, nails, or varnish between them, that is less important. Greeted and departed. Welcome and gone. Aha.

Or pocks at mare-time. You'll have to instruct me better about that, I know nothing about that. What are they, mares? They are horses. And mare-time? Is horse-time. Special horses? No, not special, heavy horses and short manes. Perhaps shaft-horses. Can they manoeuver? No. No crooked roads? No, no crooked roads. Poor horses! Poor horses? How are their ears? High but already gray. Pointed towards the top, that helps out in deafness. Does it create self-reliance? Little. But the hooves. Yes, the hooves are the chief point. Too heavy? Perhaps too heavy. Does that pull them down? It pulls them down sharply. And every horse? Almost every one. But the pocks? The pocks? I was thinking about the mares. What about the mares? I meant the manes. Oh, well they are thin; also short, as I have already said. They are always falling out. Because of beetles? No, it's just a lightness, the street is covered

73

over with mane hairs as if by hemp. And is mane hair useful for ropes? They break easily. But that's bad for the population. For whom? I think that is bad. It's bad. One slips easily on it, falls head over heels and so forth. Who falls head over heels? The horses which go over it, with their shaft poles. Do they try to get up again? They try. And do they succeed? Not all. Thus a tangle develops on earth and beyond. Then come the pocks. Up to there! Up to then the shaft poles break too, everything gets out of place differently than in the normal direction. Lucky that they are mares. Lucky? With their increasingly skinny ribs. I mean, would it not be possible to strip the pocks off to the side? To the dry Scots firs left and right? There are no Scots firs there. Now forgive the curious question, what color do pocks have? They are black. Wouldn't it be possible to alter the whole thing? Alter? I mean: pocks at mare-time. Didn't that turn out? That would be worth considering.

Let's try again with little Edison who is lolling about in our shed. He had taken along three blue pencils from his box and he is now carrying them with him. He is drawing on the barrel staves with them. What is he drawing? First three pencils, pencils are difficult to draw. Whoever doesn't know this yet, one must dissuade. Whoever knows this must go on ahead. Difficult to draw, then what? Begun from the point: everything. The edges, the six corners, sometimes eight, the length. In addition oppressed by cobwebs and dampness, perhaps also by sleep. And always the blue in his eye. One must be able to think that out. Why doesn't little Edison go home? Now he's already here. Not too much display with steps. At the sight of the Nile and the other rivers behind the knot-holes: only the necessary movements. He doesn't see the Nile at all. No, he doesn't see the Nile. But give him time. His mother is waiting and the hungry Egyptians. There is still much about which little Edison can't dream anything. Maybe we'll take him.

DOVES AND WOLVES

GIRL: Good evening.

SECTARIAN (*arranging food on an old dark dining table*): Good evening.

GIRL: I was ordered here.

SECTARIAN: Do you have the card with you?

GIRL: Yes, it was written on it. (*She begins to look, rummages in her pocket book, eventually finds the card.*) Here!

SECTARIAN: Many forget it you see. That creates difficulties.

GIRL: No, not I.

SECTARIAN: You are to receive a box of food.

GIRL: Yes?

SECTARIAN: And also something woolen.

GIRL: That's good. It's still cold anyway.

SECTARIAN: You might have been able to receive it earlier but I get the things from California. They are often late.

WIFE OF SECTARIAN (*from the next room*): Are you now finished with everything, Friedrich?

SECTARIAN: With everything.

WIFE: And soon?

SECTARIAN: Soon.

GIRL: I didn't think I would get anything at all.

SECTARIAN: Our central office is in California.

GIRL: I don't know anyone in California either.

SECTARIAN: The central office doesn't make the choice.

GIRL: Oh I see.

SECTARIAN: I make the choice.

WIFE: Will you soon be finished, Friedrich?

SECTARIAN: Soon.

WIFE: Hurry but don't rush!

GIRL (*distressed*): I don't know you either.

SECTARIAN: Are you indigent?

GIRL: Yes indeed.

SECTARIAN: That's sufficient reason.

GIRL: But —

SECTARIAN (*while he ties the box*): The contents of the box: two kilos of rice, three chocolate bars, it can also be used for chocolate drink, four cans of condensed milk, a woolen vest.

GIRL: Thank you very much!

SECTARIAN: Our central office is in California.

WIFE: Finished Friedrich?

SECTARIAN: Right away. (*To the girl.*) My wife runs a poultry farm.

WIFE: It's nearly three.

SECTARIAN: We always go out after three.

GIRL: Poultry?

SECTARIAN: Yes. Rare birds: doves with white spurs, pheasants, all kinds of poultry. Once we had an ostrich too.

GIRL: An ostrich?

SECTARIAN: Come with us if you like?

GIRL: (*hesitates*).

SECTARIAN: I think you want to go to the streetcar.

GIRL: Yes.

SECTARIAN: It's on the way. (*Into the next room.*) Are you coming Leonie?

WIFE: I am coming.

> *In front of the house then further on the way to the poultry farm.*

GIRL: I still don't know, why —

SECTARIAN: Allow me to take the box for you for a while!

WIFE: A windy day today.

GIRL: When I used to ride past here frequently —

SECTARIAN: By train of course?

GIRL: Yes. By train. And then I noticed your house, somewhat to the side next to the tile factory, with white curtains at the windows, with the fence — (*When the two others remain silent, somewhat helplessly*) — because it is so small — (*When the two others still remain silent.*) When one rides past it it appears as if one could live well in it, only —

WIFE (*sharply*): Only?

GIRL: From the train one sees the river and the house. And then one thinks one would have to see the river and the train from the house.

WIFE: One sees only the train.

GIRL: Yes. *(As if she were coming to.)* But I wanted to say something different.

SECTARIAN: We turn in here now.

GIRL: I wanted to ask —

WIFE: Here we are at the charcoal pits.

GIRL: I saw your house from the train because I was riding to work and home from work. And sometimes I thought: One could live nicely here. But it can't be that that's the reason you — *(Hesitates)* the reason that I — *(Looks at the box out of the corner of her eye)*.

SECTARIAN: You certainly also saw the charcoal pits.

GIRL *(despondently)*: Yes.

WIFE: Our farm lies right in the middle of them.

GIRL *(remains silent)*.

WIFE: One would hardly guess that it did.

GIRL *(again as in sleep like before when she spoke about the river)*: Once I saw a white dove fly over the hills of coal. It circled for a while, flew in a large arc and turned around again. Then I wondered, I thought, how —

WIFE *(quickly)*: It belonged of course to us.

GIRL: Yes, possibly.

WIFE: They all do that in the beginning.

GIRL: In the beginning?

WIFE: No one can prevent them from flying over the coal pits and soiling their wings.

SECTARIAN: Many of them even fly to the other side of the river to the poor houses over there.

WIFE: We cannot spread a net under the sky.

SECTARIAN *(laughs)*: It would not be worth the trouble either!

WIFE: Later they stop of their own accord.

SECTARIAN *(calmly)*: Later.

WIFE: Then they notice that our grains are better than the coal dust which constantly crunches under one's feet here.

SECTARIAN: Than the sand between the roof shingles over there.

GIRL *(with uncertainty)*: I can imagine that they are better.

WIFE: Yes, isn't that so? It is easy to imagine.

Screaming up from the river.

GIRL: What is that?

WIFE: Nothing.

ELIZA, ELIZA

On the fan in front of the house a family had sat down. The younger of their two daughters was sitting on the edge of the fan and was letting her legs hang in the air while the older one attempted to step over the staves without damaging the silk. From time to time two servants stepped out of the house gate, watched silently for a while what was going on, and requested the four people to leave the fan. Then the mother called, "Eliza," over from the handle next to which she was sitting and polishing, but since neither of the girls lifted their heads one didn't even know whether one of them was named that. "Eliza," the mother called again. The servants went back into the house, but after a few moments came out again and began to complain. The father of the family lifted both arms defensively and became absorbed again instantly in the small piece of writing which he held on his knees. The servants went into the house once more, and afterwards when they came back out again, attempted to chase the family from the fan with orders and threats. But that too was in vain. Father and mother didn't look up, and one of the girls, the older one, said while pointing to the father with her chin: "He has started to read for the thousandth time." "What is that?" the two servants called, while a slight breeze started up. "That's always the same," called the older girl, "that's always the very same!" Thereupon the two servants went back into the house.

All along, the lady whom they served was standing at a window of her house in the second floor and was watching. She was a heavy person with coal-black hair which she wore piled up on her head in the fashion of an earlier century. Of a century? No, more exactly: of the second half of the seventh. In her family a fashion magazine from this century had continued to be handed down until one evening it had disintegrated into dust in her hands. Ever since, she had worn the hairdo, for that was the only thing that still could clearly be seen before she moved her hands and it all decomposed: a lady unlike her otherwise, but with the same hairdo. She was guided by this picture in dust, and put forth any effort to do so. It was also not certain for what reason she should otherwise put forth any sort of effort for she had no father, no child and not even a cousin. Her family had renounced the gods before the birth of her grandfather. She had never had any idea of blaming them for it. To you and yours, unknown yet polite people wrote many times, and she read it as seriously as she took it. I and my family, I and no gods. She was always polite enough, in conversation with herself, changing the lack of presentiment of strangers into necessary awareness. She was shy with her servants and therefore had given them no instructions. Now they were making threats and were lamenting without any instructions, and one of them was walking around the fan and was touching the younger girl on the knee. But the girl didn't look up.

The fan lay on a loose stand of black, shining wood which had been constructed a long time ago especially for it. Each of its ribs corresponded to a notch in the stand, and the handle had a bed. It was not the most beautiful of all fans of its mistress, even if one of the most beautiful, but it was the widest and the most difficult to take over the back stairs into the garden. Its broad and somewhat awkward form indicated that it must have originated shortly before the beginning of the third period (there were in all four up to now) during which time among fan makers the inner sense for the proportions of the ribs had begun to decline. But precisely its proportions, which every expert felt to be slightly exaggerated and even so to be noble, gave it its value among the connoisseurs of the experts, and therefore she loved it too, somewhat more than all the other fans which she owned.

How she had gotten the idea on this afternoon to have the fan carried onto the street she didn't know. It was a quiet sandy day, the adults were still sleeping in the houses and the children in the meadows, and she then had thought to herself, "So be it" or "they won't be moving for a while!" She had also even been proud of her idea inasmuch as she allowed herself any pride. And she had noticed how good her golden fan (yes, it was golden or of a very light yellow anyway) had looked on the street, between the low houses, lowered wooden shutters, sidewalks which weren't equal to its symmetry. It wasn't necessary for it, as it was for the other fans, to be delicately stuck in between the still somewhat bare branches of the apple trees as soon as March came, and with it the time to air out all of the fans. Here a red and there a violet, here a freshly painted branch in the background and there an old garden ball delicately pressed into place, she had thought with scorn, no, hers down there didn't need that, even if all the others belonged to her also. But this one was more hers than the rest. She had gotten thus far in her thoughts, probably being enchanted by the protracted view of the rare and undissembled proportions and in an attack of inner wantoness, when she decided from now on not to have the fan brought into the garden any longer in March. The street was its realm, here it should flourish or be aired out or whatever you wanted to call it. Every March. Didn't everything concur with her? The sleepy neighbors, the sleepy children, and at the end, the still brownish grassy slopes, and the little sand clouds that arose from time to time. Was it not the only one which tolerated some sand and could be cleaned by it? Her fear that it and its stand could be touched, grazed or even be injured by thrown rocks, had vanished. Wasn't it able to lull its enemies to sleep?

Suddenly she noticed the family on the fan. She couldn't say how they had gotten up there, she hadn't turned her eyes away from it for a moment. And everything had been just the same as it was now, and as it seemed it was going to continue to be, due to the servants' laments and threats which were gradually changing into abusive shouts. The father was sitting approximately, perhaps even exactly, on the middle of the fan and was reading, the younger girl was letting her legs hang over the edge, the older one was dancing on the staves and the mother was polishing the handle. While the initial, more cautious and astonished complaints and pleas had brought them to the point of impatient movement and even to words, now nothing changed any more. The father appeared to have found the two pages he wanted to read, and his oiled hair was glistening up in this direction, struck by the spring sun. The two servants were trying to lift up the fan by the handle. From time to time they ran into the house and fortified themselves with hot wine, which stood in little mugs on the tiles on the back wall of the entrance hall. Their attempts became rougher and more violent. Anger and weakness had seized them. Their mistress was still quietly standing in the meantime behind the window and was watching.

The four people on the fan were a trace smaller and weaker than people usually are, but this trace was only measurable in terms of intimations, dependent perhaps upon the angle of observation or upon the lighting, and one could easily be mistaken about it. Even if after a period of observation it was difficult to be entirely mistaken about the illusion. If one looked directly at it then one soon had the impression that they were also flatter and again only by a trace. Their arms didn't have quite the roundness, their back didn't have quite the breadth, and it could even be that they were put together from newspaper, perhaps even from firmer pages which had dried out and which crackled with every movement. How pretty, thought the lady, how well put together! And she smiled as she explained in an imaginary conversation at tea to an imaginary friend: "What clever craftsmen there are, they can do anything! Mountains, hills, the sea and the light, round shoulders and everything out of paper. Even if easily shattered. At the beginning of a fall festival I saw...." Then she lost the thread of the imaginary conversation, and she smiled again. Her two servants were sitting on the left side of the entrance and could no longer stand on their feet. Occasionally one stuck his arm out and moved the fan but only very weakly and without any clear hope. "If it had been painted," babbled the second one, as if he were speaking of a dead man, "it would have had a pattern on it like others, people taking walks, balls, friendly people, but it was only blank." "Well I like the patterns that don't stand up." "It must be the gold, the color of daylight, this god-forsaken brightness." Their conversation did not develop further.

"Eliza," said the father, "now we'll build the ship." The older girl turned around, jumped onto the middle of the fan and stopped right in front of her father. She spread her arms like sails over her head and clasped her hands in an overlapping fashion. The mother stopped polishing, let her cloth fall onto the street over the edge of the black stand and took the handle of the fan into her hands. "It is turning," she said happily, "it is turning." "Eliza," said the father and banged his book shut, "now I am going to get the blessing down." He raised his head and saw the protruding roof of the house with some objects of crude ornamentation. "Do you get it from there?" his wife asked anxiously. "Easily," he replied and began to pray: "Oh discreet wood, rounded rafter, cracking varnish in which truth is preserved as it is everywhere, cast down upon this ship the joys of ships, protect its journey from pleasure and let it end in fire as is fitting for it." "Yes," said the mother. The younger girl had drawn her shoulders in somewhat and was stirring the sandy air with her toes. "Eliza, lamb," said the father affectionately, "join in." "Yes, baby," called the mother, "cook us some air-flakes, clean the salt from the staves, just do something." But the girl did not turn around. She shrugged her shoulders at the word air-flakes and her hair separated over her back. "There we are again," whispered the mother, "held back, held back." Tears came to her eyes. "That's the way it always is. Do you remember when we were resting in the treetops? She is resisting the boat trip!" "Eliza," the father called plaintively and the older girl near him clapped her hands impatiently and then clasped them together again over her head.

The lady opened the window above them and said with her calm voice: "These staves must not be cleaned with salt. If it were sugar and egg I would agree with you, but not salt, nothing which belongs to the many oceans and which brings disturbance to the villages." "Or rather which brings peace," she added thoughtfully after a while, and as she was leaning somewhat out of the window: "I come from a salt village. It lies on a dry hill and is now empty. But formerly there was a day of frightful disturbance. Even the cows were loaded down in order to escape the salt. My favorite cow was, with the wash tubs of the family. My little brother drove the chickens to the river where they drowned with great noise. All without heads. And the pictures," she said brightly, "we had a lot of pictures when the salt blew into the frames and they burst out with a crack. Not to mention the beds." She interrupted herself because not one of the fan people even looked up at her. "Eliza," the father repeated plaintively, "Give us some consideration." But his youngest didn't move. "We had wonderful bedclothes," the lady continued, "the edges painted with anemones." She closed the window softly, left her room, gathered up the skirt of her dress and climbed down the stairs. Then she stepped past her servants through the open house gate and walked around the fan and its stand until she was standing in the middle of the street before the youngest girl.

"Do you remember, Eliza," she said, "do you remember? How the wind struck us and how the ships howled? How the wall on the left side blew up and we thought the salt was sand? How the temple bells began to ring, how you laughed?" The girl stared rigidly past her. Whoever had made her, must have made her hair first, in the few good moments during which one is not disturbed and thinks that it will remain that way always. Her hair was the best, it started out at the hairline cautiously and thickly and fell towards the back smoothly. But her facial features were weak and only hinted at, and above her temples there ran black bands somewhat blotted out as if the news accounts to which she owed her existence could still be understood. The lady actually read, "Midday storm extinguishes...," but she quickly took her eyes away from the place and fixed them sympathetically upon the fragile figure of the little girl. "Wasn't it fun, Eliza," she repeated more softly, "when you gathered the sheep around you and played the circle game with them? And when one after the other flew into the sea, but did so happily? Your favorite with the black bow first. And the wolves from the forest right after. I have always said that wolves are curious," she continued eagerly, "only a little more curious than the rest. Then it was proved true again. But you had never wanted to believe me when I was often still sitting in the dark next to your bed, and the fragrance of peppermint tea lingered throughout the house. No, no, no, I still hear you calling with your shrill voice, child!" "What is she saying there?" one of the two servants at the entrance said, and rubbed his eyes. "I was just dreaming...." "Oh, stop it," said the other, "I can't listen." "How pigheaded you were," the lady continued urgently and without raising her voice," at that time in the old nights. And how your legs always rustled under the covers, do you remember? Like tinder. Gifted with just a little presentiment, one might have been able to predict all of the salt. And do you still remember how the sky fell in? How the bridges which they had stretched across the bay came crashing down with thousands of people on them, really with thousands of people, remember, Eliza? We were standing opposite each other in the front room where the drapes were not yet opened, and we had propped our hands on the table top and were smiling at each other, until they pulled me away from you, off into the howling plains and onto the bursting bridges. It was the neighbor with his uprooted rhododendrons in his arm. Too bad about the little girl, he said and already had me by the collar. I kicked him in the side but it didn't help. In front of him I had to carry his trifling plants of which he had much too many. I don't know whether or not you looked after us, Eliza, but I hope not. It would not have been a particularly nice view: he with his thin shoulders and loosely hanging coat, and I in front of him with the roots of determination in my arm. But since I know you, you didn't move from the table either, didn't once take your hands from the table top, did you?" A gust of wind came from the withered meadows and shook Eliza's head. "Here I am now," the lady said hesitantly in conclusion, "he was soon blown away from me and landed in another part of the city where he gives harp lessons while his rhododendrons were meandering down the rivers between the salt, they adorn the pilot station now. And you," she asked shyly, "how did you continue to fare when I was out there? What happened? What did you do?" The girl began to move the air with her feet again while the half-finished sentence on her temple became clearer in the sinking light. "Eliza," the mother said softly, "don't stir up the sand, how will our ship look when we are about to take off?" "With its new coat of paint," she added lamenting. "I must know before the neighbors on the left and on the right wake up," whispered the lady, and bent down close to the child, "do tell me, did you still make tea when I was out there, did you decorate the green foundling? Or did you not move your hands from the table until today?" "I don't expect you did," she said, "and they had to spread the cloth for tea daily over your tapering fingers and move the cake plate to the wrong side." She laughed. "But tell me,

Eliza, tell me what happened to you when the salt settled? For I know as little now as I did when I was still on the bridge with my shadow and that of the rhododendron above the blocks shoving against each other in the river!" Eliza was silent and held her legs still. "Or did someone disturb you? Who was it who rushed in and saddled you with plans?"

"It wasn't I, Eliza," the older one called while a shadow of red rushed to her neck, "was it, it wasn't I?" "The official's little daughter searches for the first bird and so forth," said the lady, without paying her any attention, "who wrote the old verses in your notebook or did no one write them?" "He has begun again to read for the thousandth time," called the older daughter and pointed to the father who was holding a page of his book up with two fingers.

"Reading a thousand times," murmured the lady scornfully, and propped herself up on a stave of her fan while she said that, "it's a good thing but your father carries it too far. Follow your neighbor, was one of my first sentences, and I would like to have known which one, but I never found out. Nevertheless already by the ninety-third time some things dawned on me. Yes, just think, Eliza, it dawned on me. And now I am also here. I have two servants and a house, on the roof's ridge of which on five days of the year some snow settles, a swimming pool over the outer rim of which the lines of the yearly flight of ducks go, here I am, at least I am not giving harp lessons. No, no, not that, even if I am getting a little chatty as time goes by. My little dove ..." she said and bent over to Eliza shocked, for from the outside corners of her eyes tears began to roll down in big drops while the mother struggled in vain to get back her cloth from the street in between the staves of the black stand, "don't cry, my little dove, it would ruin the unfinished news accounts on your cheeks!" "Help her," she then said sternly to the servants looking out over Eliza. The two servants jumped up, the first of them fetched the cloth, shook it out and handed it to the woman on the fan. They leaned back morosely against the house wall, but didn't dare to sit down against it again. The woman on the fan was about to start polishing the handle again. She stopped at a signal from her husband, lifted her head and said: "How is it going with the boat trip?" "I mean how are you?" "Oh there are the most varied kinds of things to keep in mind," replied the lady in a distraught manner, "from the white lacquer to the timbers of the bow—Eliza," she called, kneeled down in the middle of the street and embraced the legs of the little girl, "dry your tears." "They will wake the neighbors, they will blot the news reports, they will do everything to defy us." "Or tell

me at least why you are crying." "Because I left you, child?"
"Believe me, when I was walking through the front garden and
saw the uncertain cloud over me with its lifeless forms I was
already sorry and I thought: How can I leave Eliza behind, will she
discover the half glass of milk on the piano? And the questions
soon got sharper. "Eliza," she called, "it's snowing!"

In fact it had begun to snow from the sky which was almost
clear, and an old dirty man stuck his head out of the house door
diagonally opposite and said: "Your time is coming children!"
"Did you hear, Eliza," said the lady impatiently. "Leave your
darling there," called the old man at an angle across the street,
"nothing will happen to her!" "I have already heard that once,"
said the lady, "and I don't want to hear it again." She put her silk
cloth around her head, pulled the stand which ran on wheels, with
the fan and the people into the middle of the street and signaled to
her servants. To the left and to the right windows and doors were
opened and neighbors and neighbors' children looked out of the
light frames curiously while the lady pulled her fan through the
whirl of snow and the misty light to the hills. On the first rise of a
hill she stopped and could still just see the rim of the swimming
pool sparkling up from the apple garden. "If you would now like
to assist with the boat trip?" said the woman on the fan. "I do
want to assist with the boat trip," replied the lady and began to
pull again. The servants were pushing. The people on the fan kept
silent.

Shortly before the last rounded hill-top the lady felt her fan
suddenly becoming heavy. She turned around and saw her two ser-
vants running like shadows across the meadows towards the city.
From time to time they turned around and sent mocking or im-
ploring gestures up to her. She watched them for some moments
and compared them in her heart with gray shutters which belonged
to a tower, but the slope at this place was too steep for a rest, and
she had to go on. She tugged and she heard the stand crack behind
her and its little rollers give a jolt over a stone. In a valley at the
bottom of the hill a snow rabbit was sitting. She still saw it. Then
she heard herself being called. She heard the faint voice almost
stifled with laughter which called her by name. Once and again.
She turned around rapidly. But neither the slope of the road nor
her strength were a match for this turn since she had already
started up to the peak along the snake-like path. The stand began
to roll and pulled her along. She saw the city already speeding
back towards her, her servants, her swimming pool— how did her
apple garden look in the angry turmoil?—then the fan loosed itself
from the stand with its cargo and was carried by a whirlwind into

the air. The lady succeeded in clinging to one of the unnecessary side straps, a product of the weakened style, and drew herself up onto it. The fan swayed, fell a little, stretched out and glided towards the coast.

The lady seized the two slender, wet arms which had helped her and perhaps she took hold of them too firmly. The arms folded up under her hands, the neck folded, shoulders, head and knee, and what she held after all was a page of newspaper, torn and breaking apart at the many folds, with some thick black letters at the head, which were already running together and were imparting nothing any more other than their own terror, and under them, three hurried columns running diagonally, the center one somewhat thicker, which the snow was blotting out. "A folding game!" called the older girl and clapped her hands, "I knew it right away." "Come to my heart," called the mother on the fan and extended her arms out towards the lady. "My daughter," the father said and lifted his head from the book.

The snow disappeared, the sun came out. Far down below one saw the white page, the folding game undone and fluttering quickly towards the water. The lady bent down and made everything sway again. "Old news reports," the father said behind her with his calm voice, "an old newspaper on which we were practicing." "She called me by name," the lady on the fan replied.

DOVER

Warld would be better than world. Less useful, less apt. Orth would be better than earth. But this is the way it is now. Normandy is called Normandy and nothing else. The rest also. Everything is arranged to suit. To suit each other, as one says. And as one sees too. And as one doesn't see either. Only Dover is not to be improved upon. Dover is called just as it is. All designations and that which they designate are to be revolutionized from this, as many people say, place of little importance. Delft, Hindustan, also beyond. Although beyond is not a place. Or probably not a place. But Dover, persistent and very much on edge doesn't use its power. That is precisely its sign of excellence. Whoever changes trains there, looks about hastily and notices nothing. Dover, incorruptible and quiet between snares and imperfections, doesn't cause a very big stir. Chalk cliffs and one or two lullabyes from one or two wars: one can pursue modesty no further. To perish in Dover is almost as easy as in Calcutta with its pestilence and its poorly invented name, its hot smoke. One can learn in Dover as well as anywhere to walk stooped over, to rage wildly, to skip. But only away from Dover does it remain clear and unpretentious for the one who masters it. He can later move away, operate carousels, build writing rooms—what he picked up in Dover he doesn't lose, what he became in Dover, someone stooped over, a wild person, a clown, makes him unfit for felling. Annie, for example, who had learned only to slaver in Dover, because she came away from there at an early age, is still master of it in Denver where she landed at age ninety in an asylum, to a degree which made the attendants tremble with envy and angry amazement when moving her to another bed. And while still trembling they noticed that their trembling corresponded only to its lack-lustre designation and not to that which it was. None of them had learned it in Dover. Nevertheless they had an inkling. In this way Dover spreads exact inklings. Neither air nor water can prevent it from doing that, nor can the earth. And not its own chalk either. Dover can meddle with dispositions without their having a harmful effect upon it. With little white cots. With Johnnys in them, with red-cheeked Marys, Dawns, Deans. With everything that is aimed at beyond. Even with colors in general, few as there are. But Dover doesn't spread a theory of colors, no knowledge. The attendants in Denver will never find out what made them tremble. The few sailors who have run aground in Dover do not know, when they get stranded next time on more distant and more likely places, how they deserve the desperate admiration of their comrades.

Whoever would like to chat with Marlowe on a gloomy Sunday, step upon the lyre of Wilde or sketch a house in Tudor style, one to one, should fix his gaze instantly on Dover. He will not meet Marlowe there, not find Wilde's harp, and will soon consider Tudor style irrelevant. He will sum up his wishes rapidly and exactly, he will want to play with pebbles, he will build a pebble playground, rather high up, near the cliffs, he will take a long time but he will learn like no other how to play with pebbles, how to get at them with fingers and feet, to restrain them. He will become the pebble player about whom the world speaks. He will become unfit for felling sooner than Annie in Denver. Dover has brought his wishes to their senses, Dover will have brought them to their senses, let us say. Or to rest. Pebble for pebble. Look at him up there how he bends over to them. Tenderly as no other. He is correct.

Besides everyone knows that one gets to know the world in chalk stores. That is said incidentally but speaking incidentally wants to be learned also. And whoever has not learned it in Dover will have a difficult time. He will fall back again and again into the main thought in spite of every effort and it will depress him. Then he will meet the one who was supposed to give a speech on King Arthur's roundtable at the cliff school and never accomplished it—who was never called on again and therefore began to speak incidentally. About interstices, cap cords, uninteresting stuff. That's the one who will beat him for good. But they do have to do with each other, at least to some extent. Dover remains in the game.

Why do we observe our moments, if not in Dover? Why do we value them greatly or little, do they allow us to steal or not? And how? How do you spend a moment that lies yet before you and yet is once and for all lost? We wish to be silent about those which we have passed, those which lie behind us. How can we forget to say it recently and later, even at this very instant? How if not here? Everything in Dover. Dover is acquainted with the multiplicity of the disciplines which serve moments. In the moving air above the cliffs hover increasingly the faculties, the front and rear entrances, towers and flat buildings, camps, hiding places, possibilities of flight. Here one can train his dreams inside and out and let them down into wells dug recently and especially for them. Here one is clear about the fact that what is attacked is always the moment. The affinities between walking crooked, at an angle and straight are correctly set. Do you want more?

No, no there should not be a third lullabye on Dover. That was always a way to the hecatombs and Dover leaves out the hecatombs. It is set on little crowds, on the slightest ones, on rapid depreciations.

And how is it with friendships made in Dover? Do they stand firm or do they dissolve confronted with the well-known measurements? It is this way or that. Dover does not rely on friendships. It has its slaverers, its rope jumpers, its pebble players and rarely stranded crews. It's this way or that with friendships in Dover, you have to take that in the bargain. And if it is this way or that, then Dover will entreat for us: Denver, Trouville and Bilboa. It will entreat the places of the world for us with its easy glances. It will keep its eyes focused on the asylum of Privas and the other asylums too. It won't leave out that by which it cannot be measured, it will make use of its weaknesses and its weakness. It also will not forget industry, assiduity, simplicity and the fact that everything will soon be used up. It will not shove aside failed desperation which is ours. Not Dover.

WHITE CHRYSANTHEMUMS

GENERAL *(an old man)*: We should order coal.

GENERAL'S WIFE: I am waiting for the woman who is bringing me flowers. White chrysanthemums for the graves. I discovered a new flower shop, not large but respectable. They'll come to the house.

GENERAL: White chrysanthemums?

GENERAL'S WIFE: Yes, for the graves.

GENERAL: Everything is thought of here: White chrysanthemums for the graves, pears for canning, feathers for pillows, they must be refilled!

GENERAL'S WIFE: I don't understand you.

GENERAL: They are all being ordered: apple-women, pear-women, flower-women. All for diversion.

GENERAL'S WIFE: From what?

GENERAL: From the men who are supposed to bring the coal. Every year coal is ordered too late in our house, we always miss the fixed day and pay too much. And if it depended on you: there wouldn't be any coal ordered at all.

GENERAL'S WIFE: Only since the coal store was taken over by this woman; I have an aversion to her.

GENERAL: Taken over by the woman?

GENERAL'S WIFE: Yes, the man died.

GENERAL: I didn't know that.

GENERAL'S WIFE: There isn't another store in the vicinity.

GENERAL: I'm going there now. I know neither the woman nor the man well, but I want to be warm when winter comes.

GENERAL'S WIFE: Calm down!

GENERAL: And I want to take a walk. I was just thinking about where to go.

GENERAL'S WIFE: Besides today is Sunday.

GENERAL: Sunday? And your flower-woman?

GENERAL'S WIFE: She comes even on Sunday. That's just it.

GENERAL: Yes? Don't taxis run on Sunday? Why don't you take

one, be driven to the train and come home on foot? Why not? I am amazed! If kindergartens were open today I think you would announce ten little children that don't exist. Just from sympathy. But you don't order coal. Because it's not open on Sunday or you don't like the woman.

GENERAL'S WIFE: Because I don't like the woman. But I'll go tomorrow.

GENERAL: Tomorrow we'll pay more, tomorrow the fixed day will be past. Today is winter, already today do you hear?

A bell rings outside.

GENERAL'S WIFE *(with excitement)*: That will be the flower-woman. *(She goes out to open the door.)*

GENERAL: White chrysanthemums!

GENERAL'S WIFE *(reenters with the flower-woman)*: This is the nice friendly flower-woman, dear, about whom I told you. And whether or not you want to believe it, you see now: she comes on Sundays too! She comes to the house. Up to the fifth floor.

GENERAL: There are so many!

FLOWER-WOMAN: White chrysanthemums.

GENERAL: I wasn't expecting anything else.

GENERAL'S WIFE: That is correct, my dear woman, that is fine, what you are bringing us! That will give the right appearance to the graves more than ever.

GENERAL: Our graves would have the proper appearance anyway, even without chrysanthemums. Even if only the green grass were over them, even if only bare earth —

GENERAL'S WIFE: But this way they'll have more of a respectable appearance.

GENERAL *(angrily)*: That's enough now.

FLOWER-WOMAN: May I put the flowers here? *(Points to a dark corner of the room.)*

GENERAL'S WIFE: Certainly, my dear. *(Enraptured.)* How they do gleem!

FLOWER-WOMAN: Yes, they are pretty. But they should not be where it's too warm.

GENERAL: They'll not get too warm.

GENERAL'S WIFE: We'll certainly see to that.

FLOWER-WOMAN: Otherwise we don't guarantee that they'll still be fresh and radiant on the day fixed for floral decoration.

GENERAL: On which fixed day?

GENERAL'S WIFE *(beaming)*: Fixed for floral decoration.

GENERAL: St. Valentine?

GENERAL'S WIFE: No! Dear, please understand: the day fixed for floral decoration.

GENERAL: That's a surprise to me.

GENERAL'S WIFE: Right?

GENERAL: It coincides with the day for coal.

GENERAL'S WIFE: It's not every year, only every — *(Looks inquiringly over at the flower-woman.)*

FLOWER-WOMAN: Every seventy, eighty years.

GENERAL'S WIFE: That's why not everyone knows about it either.

GENERAL: No, those who die at the age of five don't.

GENERAL'S WIFE: And therefore I thought —

GENERAL *(sharply)*: What?

GENERAL'S WIFE: That we should use it. That we should decorate the graves as long as there is time: the graves of our grandparents and parents, all of our nearer relatives, all of our — *(Catches her breath.)*

GENERAL: You thought of that?

GENERAL'S WIFE: Yes. And not only about that. *(Smiles roguishly.)* I thought we could if possible now decorate our own graves.

GENERAL: Yes?

GENERAL'S WIFE: Yes, dear.

GENERAL: We would have to be lying in them to do this.

GENERAL'S WIFE: Not right away we wouldn't. We would have to only within — *(Looks again inquiringly over at the flower-woman.)*

FLOWER-WOMAN: Three weeks.

GENERAL'S WIFE: Quite right. Three weeks.

FLOWER-WOMAN: But any day earlier is better.

GENERAL: I understand that.

GENERAL'S WIFE: Naturally. What do you think, can we perhaps already have everything in fourteen days —

GENERAL: Everything?

GENERAL'S WIFE: Exactly —

GENERAL: Why not then in eight days? Or even better in three? Or best of all today, today before noon, before all the churchgoers come home?

GENERAL'S WIFE: Dearest!

FLOWER-WOMAN *(discreetly)*: The people diagonally opposite ordered Chinese foliage plants. And those farther over near the church tulips.

GENERAL'S WIFE: Tulips!

GENERAL: They would be an idea too.

GENERAL'S WIFE: But white chrysanthemums are better. *(Anxiously to the flower-woman.)* Or?

FLOWER-WOMAN: They have it in them.

GENERAL'S WIFE *(enthusiastically)*: Do you hear?

FLOWER-WOMAN: They stay bright even when everything else becomes paler.

GENERAL: Aren't fresh ones supplied?

FLOWER-WOMAN: Yes. But the flowers must be taken out soon so that they remain damp.

GENERAL'S WIFE: We'll go right away!

FLOWER-WOMAN: If possible three days before the burial.

GENERAL: We are going to die right away.

FLOWER-WOMAN: Then just a half day earlier.

GENERAL'S WIFE: How do the others do it?

FLOWER-WOMAN: Most people take a taxi out directly. Some go by bus and transfer to the streetcar, but the least —

GENERAL'S WIFE: Dear, let's go right away! It is Sunday and I am worried that the few taxis in the vicinity will all be taken.

GENERAL *(calmly)*: Right now?

GENERAL'S WIFE: Yes, right away. We'll eat lunch late, put our things in order —

GENERAL: And die about six?

GENERAL'S WIFE: That's what I thought.

GENERAL: If I correctly understand it, our street wants to die because of this fixed day for flower decoration?

FLOWER-WOMAN: Some people have already decided, even if by no means all.

GENERAL: I am surprised about that.

GENERAL'S WIFE: I am too.

FLOWER-WOMAN: The most beautiful graves are awarded prizes.

GENERAL: That's already clear to me.

GENERAL'S WIFE: Which families have already decided?

FLOWER-WOMAN: I am not permitted to name them.

GENERAL'S WIFE: Do you hear? Best if we decided immediately! If

SELECTED POETRY AND PROSE

we hesitate, all the others will be ahead of us.

GENERAL: Yes. Then they'll be ahead of us.

GENERAL'S WIFE *(enthusiastically)*: It's up to us, Alfred.

GENERAL: One more question.

FLOWER-WOMAN: A question?

GENERAL: It's about the cloudiness over the cemeteries.

FLOWER-WOMAN *(who has become paler)*: The cloudiness over the cemeteries?

GENERAL: I mean: on the day fixed for flower decoration, on this day after our death. *(Without letting her answer.)* Will the cloudiness be mignonette color, pink or pale green?

FLOWER-WOMAN: Mignonette color, pink or pale green?

GENERAL *(more sharply)*: I am asking: How will the sky be? Damp, blue-gray, similar to street pavement in twilight or to feathers of doves which make a brief ascent on the church square in the morning?

FLOWER-WOMAN: Similar to street pavement at twilight or feathers of doves?

GENERAL *(steps up to her)*: I am asking. And I say to you: You know the answer. It will be red, the sky, hacked to pieces and boiling!

FLOWER-WOMAN: I know nothing. I can say nothing, I —

GENERAL: Get out now!

Flowers and flower-woman disappear, two bright somewhat pink spots from the sun are seen on the parquet.

GENERAL'S WIFE *(to the General)*: Where are you going?

GENERAL: To order the coal. Besides, I still want to feed the doves on the church square.

THE GUEST

Adolphe visits his aunts twice a year. There are people who think he visits them twice a week but that is a misleading thought. He visits them twice a year. He acts then to be sure as if he visited them almost daily, takes along their house-key which he carries with him also otherwise more often than not, starts out right after school, cuts through the front garden, quickly jumps up the four or five low steps, opens the door and is at their house. He seldom brings them flowers and when he does only blue ones, a thin bouquet for both. One can say that that happens every year and a half. He brings pin-on flowers even more rarely. He doesn't dislike going to their house. In the entrance hall which has a darker effect than it would have to have because of the windows in various colors, he greets them with a loud voice. He embraces them, he tells them what has happened that morning. He never gets further back in his stories. He says: "Mr. Meyers has caught a cold. When he was talking about the Stoics during the third class he could hardly get his breath. That's the way it was." And he imitates Mr. Meyers who has caught cold. Or he says: "Anne wrote from Penzance. I'm curious how long she'll hold out in the nest. The letter was sticking in the door this morning." Anne is his sister. Then again he says: "The Stoics are difficult to keep in mind. They don't agree with me." Adolphe is not a bad conversationalist. He takes off his glasses at intervals, rubs them clean, tastes the tea and admires it. He listens to questions. He says he can well imagine that one is plagued by headaches, especially those on the side, he can imagine it well this very day. That the air was like that today, also in the classrooms. That it was not absolutely the result of the damp fur coats in the entrance hall, and also not because of being on the northeast side. This afternoon he will concern himself with the Epicureans, he thinks he can gain better access there, and in this way perhaps even remember the Stoics better. This way he brings the afternoon into the conversation. The afternoon he says always seems to him like a kind of doubt in the afternoon while the morning seems often like a kind of faith in the morning. Today that is no different either. You can see that he takes his aunts seriously, he demands something from the conversation with them. But he doesn't demand too much. "Stoa" he suddenly says, broadens the *a* excessively and laughs. He would like to know, he says, how Anne is getting along in Penzance with the mornings and afternoons. Anne is blond and that changes many things, could lead to the very opposite in questions of viewpoint. And then too Penzance is really very far west. He looks at the northeast windows in the bay with a smile. No, not even for the sake of the afternoon sun can one be too preoccupied with the west. But Anne will indeed come back. Yes, he presumes that. Penzance is simply an extravagance. Is extravagant, of course. What Adolphe says there sounds definitive but as if he didn't want to frighten his aunts, not even upset them with the presumption of a too abrupt departure, he leans back and unbuttons two buttons of his vest. And he starts right away to talk of his preference for vests, solid color, multicolored, bright and dark. He has a selection of them. And he takes care of them. Whoever wears a respectable vest, he says, can even afford to go without shoes. But naturally that is uncomfortable. Adolphe becomes silent for a moment. He guards against pursuing this subject too far. He even says so. Every subject has its dangers, he says. Asks if they too haven't already made this discovery? That is a serious interest of his. One can quite certainly make discoveries without considering them to be such. That is perhaps the more economic way of making discoveries. In the last analysis the philosophies profited from that, which one then gets presented in school. The shortened versions. The interpreters. Mr. Meyers. Adolphe becomes somewhat restless. He seems not to have avoided quickly enough the danger which every subject implies. He takes more tea. He begins to praise the color of the window frames. Peeling or not he says they were suitable. Aren't there enough window frames which have an oppressive effect, cold? He has observed that especially during ship inspections, Anne too, that time when they were still together. For Anne has been away now of course for a long time and who knows what kind of window frames she has in Penzance. Yes, that's it. Not that Anne didn't look distinguished in every frame, that isn't the question. Adolphe begins to cough, says thank you politely in between for the help offered to him, drinks some water, coughs harder, takes a piece of sugar and says thank you again. But he looks annoyed. He jumps up, goes quickly to the window, leans against the windowsill and looks out. You can look at him and see that he is looking out with effort. It is ridiculous with this cough, he says, and turns back into the room, but don't worry, something can certainly be done for it. He must not talk of boats, boat inspections, maybe not of Penzance either. Besides he has very good drops at home, quite generally calming too. Adolphe has control of himself again now. Menthol he says and best with milk. Can you imagine that: milk with menthol? This idea seems to put him in a good mood in any case. He smiles. He sits down again and remarks that girls now are frequently being named Melissa like the recently born sister of a friend. One tiny little Melissa after the other. With boys such a biased preference has yet to take place. But the thing is worth a study. These jumps from name to name. With centers of gravity without centers of gravity. And then precisely Melissa. People were racking their brains much too little over . their name preferences. That could after all be instructive and be a protection against endangerments. One often gets fool-hardy fears. What if quite generally dissimilarity of names disappeared? Improbable from the standpoint of the statisticians but indeed extremely possible. Like the carnival guilds. One should have asked a statistician before the development of carnival guilds whether there was a possibility for their origination, whether there were ways of thinking that were favorable to the thing as well as to the designation of it. Should have kept asking. What did they think he would have said? There were none he would have said: He, Adolphe, wasn't planning to become a statistician. To be more exact he would have banished it from his mind. Although it was very clear to him that his mind could change again unexpectedly. In favor of statistics. Growth of limitation, curtailment, Adolphe says, it is naturally easy to excite agreement with such alternatives just as it is with the admitted or unadmitted love for the whole thing. Adolphe laughs now as if this love were hardly to be expected of him, he laughs reluctantly, a kind of precipitous smile and he is in a hurry. He doesn't like to be in a hurry, it clearly goes against his nature. Adolphe would like to be sketched, and he is very clear about the fact that haste and smiling could harm the sketched portrait. Adolphe has his ideas of sketched portraits and not only for his own. He once saw a sketch of one who was blowing out a candle, it was a failure. Whoever puts out candles is in a hurry, is even in a big hurry. Blind passion only leads to passion for blinding. No, Adolphe knows very well that he should not be in a hurry. One day he will meet right here at the aunts' house the one who will put him down on paper. Who cannot refrain from drawing while he is watching him, Adolphe, with his legs stretched out or smiling at the window. While he is telling about Mr. Meyers and philosophy. About Melissa first names and milk with menthol. Et cetera et cetera. That all would have to be taken care of clearly. A blinking of the eye that is not necessary. The whole pretense, but not the ones that work them up into a panic. Not the ones that are not apropos. No Stifter figures, not all the way down either, not hidden beneath the frame either, as soon as one comes to the frame. Yes, yes that's the way it would have to be. That's the way it will be. Adolphe suddenly feels tired out, hides a yawn. He would like to begin again about Anne and Penzance but he won't do it. His sister Anne should stay out of the game when the game gets tired. He is annoyed. It was always like that. It is always like that. It is always the thought of his own picture which introduces the end. The thought of the pencil sketch which should match him. He takes a liqueur. And another. He delights in the desperate taste which will drive him on. His morning stories are covered over, his afternoon stories too. The good tea. He takes leave of his aunts. He does not say that he will return, he never does. Instead he says, and tries to hide his haste, he hopes that they might have a fine afternoon. Certainly in the garden or perhaps preferably inside. He hopes sincerely he hasn't stayed too long. But he couldn't praise the window frames enough, really not. He wished he found such window frames everywhere he went. They were really a life-support. Could guard one from every possible thing. He laughs. Actually. The underrated was a subject in any case. He was going to try to blend it into the major subjects. As imperceptibly as possible of course. He laughs again. Did he have something else? No, naturally not, they were the flowers of course that he had brought and they were to stay here. It was really almost the same every time. Almost every time he thought he had forgotten something that he had brought. He was impossible. And he laughs again. He can laugh safely now, with contortions, chuckling and grimacing. The one who was to catch him and put him down on paper, the sketcher, didn't come. And he won't come any more either. It was again all in vain.

MY GREEN DONKEY

I see a green donkey walk across the railroad bridge daily, its hooves clatter on the planks, its head towers over the railing. I don't know where it comes from, I was never yet able to observe that. I presume, however, from the electric plant left open on the other side of the bridge from where the street runs straight as an arrow to the northwest (a global direction of which I never could make heads or tails anyway) and in the ruined entrance of which soldiers often stand to embrace their girls as soon as it has gotten dark and there is only a weak shred of light left across the rusty roof. But my donkey comes earlier. Not as if it came already at noon or shortly thereafter when the sun's glare still burns into every single one of the abandoned courtyards over there and between the cracks of the windows nailed shut. No it comes with the first imperceptible slackening of light, then I see it, usually already up there on the footbridge or as it is climbing the stairway up to it. One single time did I see it still on the other side of the track clattering over the pavement but it appeared to be in a hurry as if it were behind time. At that time, moreover, it seemed to me as if it were coming in the heat straight out of the half-open immobile gate of the electric plant.

It is not bothered by railway employees or any other people who use the bridge, it gives them right of way courteously, and it is little concerned also by the pounding and whistling of the trains which sometimes pass through under the bridge while it is going across it. It turns its head often sideways and looks down, mostly when there is no train coming and never for very long. It seems then to me as if it is exchanging words with the tracks but that is probably not possible. And for what purpose? When it has reached the far side of the middle of the bridge then it disappears after some hesitation without turning around. I am not mistaken about that, that is, about the manner of its disappearance. I understand that completely too, why should it take the trouble to turn around, since it knows the way after all?

But how does it come, from where does it come, and where does it originate? Does it have a mother or a bed of hay in one of the quiet courtyards over there? Or does it inhabit one of the former offices and have a corner in it that is its own, a part of the wall? Or does it originate like lightning between the former high-tension poles and the lines hanging down? Of course I do not know exactly how lightning originates, I don't want to know either unless my donkey were to originate in the same fashion. My donkey? That is boasting. But I won't take it back. Certainly it is possible that others also see it but I'll not ask them. My donkey which I do not feed, do not water, the coat of which I do not rub smooth, and to which I do not give consolation. Its silhouette is outlined so indubitably against the distant mountain ranges just as the mountain ranges themselves are brought into relief against the afternoon. In my eyes, thus my donkey. Why should I not admit that I live on the moment in which it arrives? That its appearance creates air for me to breath, it alone, its outline, the shades of its green and its manner of dropping its head and of looking down at the tracks? I already thought of the fact that it might be hungry and would be looking for grasses and the sparse plants which grow between the railroad ties. But one should restrain one's sympathy. I am old enough to do so, I will not lay a bundle of hay on the bridge. It doesn't look bad, not ill-nourished not tormented—but not particularly good either. There are however to be sure few donkeys which do look particularly good. I don't want to slip back into old mistakes, I wouldn't want to demand too much of it. I want to be satisfied with expecting it or rather with not expecting it. For it doesn't come regularly. Did I forget to say? It failed to appear already twice. I write it down hesitantly for perhaps that is its rhythm, perhaps such a thing as twice doesn't exist for it at all and it did continue to come, regularly, and would be surprised at this complaint. Just as it seems to be amazed otherwise about many things. Surprise, yes, that's what characterizes the donkey best, what distinguishes it I believe. I want to learn to limit myself to conjectures which concern it alone, later even to less. But up to that point there is still much which disturbs me. More than its possible hunger for example, the fact that I don't know the location of its sleep, of its rest and with that perhaps of its birth. For it requires rest. It could even be that it requires death each time, I don't know. I consider it strenuous to go over the bridge each evening as green as that, to look like it does and to disappear at the right moment.

Such a donkey requires rest, much rest. And the question is whether an old electric plant is the correct place for it, whether it is sufficient? Whether the wire lines hanging down stroke it soft enough as soon as it is not there, during its night? For its night is longer than ours. And whether the silhouettes of the mountains show it sufficient friendliness during its day? For its day is shorter. As always, I don't know. I shall not find out either, for my goal can only be to know less and less about it, since I have already learned so much about it during the half year that it has been coming. Learned from it. And thus perhaps I shall also learn to endure it when it no longer comes, for I am afraid of that. It could fail to come because of the cold, and that could be part of its coming just as is its coming itself. Till then I want to learn so little about it that I can also endure its failure to come, so that I then no longer direct my eyes to the bridge.

But until I get that far I dream often that it could have a green father and a green mother, a bundle of hay in one of the court-yards over there and in its ears the laughter of the young people who are embracing in the entrance. That it sleeps often instead of dying.

WISCONSIN AND APPLE-RICE

Should one begin again to tell the old sentimental stories? In order to conjure up sympathy? Which direction are we travelling, Your Grace? Well, we are travelling this direction of course. Downstream. Everything appears to be up to us. Or is it? Stop, stop the questions. You admit that it is possible that green will never again be green, you have already admitted it. That the goblins are leaving us alone. They should too. The grid-lines are jumping more and more into the picture, you can certainly see that. They argue with each other and while they are arguing they jump. We remain here however. We wait and see. We wait and see what all can come from the argument. Everything possible can. Pictures, a California lady telling a story, apple-rice. We both are acquainted with that, they'll not make us weak with that. The lady tells quite a good story. Looks however as if she is teasing her little brothers. Leave her. Now here we are again making insinuations. Leave them. She is telling her tale much too loudly. You should let her. Well, good, the changeable framing becomes her. Now she is coughing. She appears heavy. A heavy lady telling a story. I tell you that is not sufficient. You will see that it is not sufficient. But it must be sufficient for us. Together with the apple-rice. Whatever comes should always be enough for us. Ladies, bound negroes. Do you know what I believe? We are saddled with that which is disavowed. They have wanted to teach us for a long time to die with a smile. I see now a monastery in Wisconsin. They are washing dishes there. To be sure very significantly. One is good also for many things there. Always this black and white. The lady from California is wearing a green blouse and a black jacket with it. I can now only still see the neck. But before she was wearing what I said. Quite sure. One should leave out sure also. All questions and all certainties. But that is difficult. We succeeded, we did. How many are we anyway? Two? Are you sure? No, no don't say anything. I know, I know. Everything wrong. But only in the presentation. The material itself is correct. The general material. How that clicks when the grid-lines shift. And they shift always when they jump. Now the lady is out, Wisconsin too, the apple-rice is left. It is tireless. It hangs in there so that it withstands

all leaps. It is completely part of it and the argument doesn't dis-
turb it. Probably lovingly and without supplying half a thought.
Good, good we must take what is offered. But then the half-moon
would have been preferable to me. Or a Greek letter for departure.
One of the middle ones. For after departure there is an odor. Of
lead, pencils. According to the circumstances. It tastes that way
too. Believe me, that was not meant for the palate from the very
start. The palate must be protected almost to the end. But now we
have the lead on our tongue and the apple-rice before our eyes.
There is the lady again. I wouldn't have thought so, really not. She
is tenacious. Do you think that she wasn't finished either with her
story-telling when she was out of the picture? I know, I know, no
questions. Captain Littlewood didn't ask any either. That's not
from me, she said that. It was naturally a little joke or should be
one. She's not too successful at that with her heavy face. Wagers
that she is holding a riding whip hidden where the frame ends. She
touches me. And that is good also. She doesn't touch you. Do you
think that Wisconsin will return, the monastery with the little dish-
washing women? No, well: Perhaps Wisconsin will come back
too, the monastery and so forth. Perhaps it will be allowed to have
a name. Perhaps it is allowed to have a name. It must be allowed to
be called that. Otherwise nothing is left. Perhaps there should be
public protection. No one has the idea. Most don't like it. No ob-
ject protects it. The lady up there has no use for it. For her every-
thing is what it is. And how it is. She has that in common with her
laughing healers. But she is alone. She can of course touch one. No
one is supposed to place her on her gloomy head, otherwise she
would fall over. And that's that. How quickly everything moves up
to us, which moves up to us. It jumps. You know that too. Too
bad that the pictures don't multiply. Again and again the lady,
Wisconsin, the apple-rice. Or maybe not bad. Or perhaps not bad
at all. Wait and see. Can be that in the last analysis with these
jumps only one of the three will join the party. Or they will all fall
together into one. The whole thing is however now already rather
close to us, don't you find? And we can no longer take many steps
back. There in the back it plunges down quite steeply. Or not.
Don't shove me, I didn't ask a question. I said: It plunges down or
not. Lucky that we are not alone. I mean none of us. Admit that it
is lucky. But you admit nothing. You are a listener, one who
sounds out others. Only occasionally do you give a shove. Now
there is another click. Quite nice and ordinary the way that clicks.
Now slowly it becomes dangerous. If the apple-rice would only
disappear, apple-rice doesn't suit me. No, no reasons. What are
reasons? What reasons are. Should I say: The apple-rice doesn't

suit me because it is ridiculous? I can indeed say it. One could get a lump of rice in the eye too if the stuff is correct. Although it doesn't look like that. It is hanging firmly inside, the apples too. Brown on the edges but nevertheless. And Wisconsin appears to be equally stable in its own way. The little monastery. I am not worried there. But to one who would ask me if we will come through again, diagonally through the grid-lines, through the small metal frames, through the empty ones of course or around outside, to him I would say: No. Now there is only one step left behind us. Or whatever you want to call it. Then nothing comes along any more and what does come foams. That unites us with Wisconsin, with the rice and with the poor lady. We have now plunged into the choice which we never had, panting, sniffing, gurgling, but we are in it. I would like to see you now. I wonder whether you are diving into the apple-rice or into the swilled-down monastery kitchen. Whether you are still humming something when it flushes you up into the air. One can hum all Federal states. Or a shred of the stuff that the lady tells us, a shred.

But she is not telling anything any more. She has stopped. That is a bad sign. And if it is not a bad sign then it is a bad sign. She left her mouth open too, half open, that looks crack-brained, she must not do that, tell her, she must not, she should keep on narrating, tell her, for all I care about Wisconsin and the apple-rice, do you hear, tell her, tell her, pull her tangled locks, pinch her cheeks, but tell her, she should keep talking. She should keep telling her tale.

THE JOUET SISTERS

I now associate only with the two Jouet sisters. They admonish me when I exaggerate. When I say *farmstead* instead of *farm*, they are there instantly. Already again, says Rosalie. She calls Anna and Josepha, we'll begin from the beginning. A *junk* says Rosalie. A *junk*, I say. *China* calls Anna. *China* I call. *Foxes* says Josepha, she is the quietest. *Josua* I say. We must begin over again. *Jonas* says Josepha. *Jonas* I say. *Jonas* says Anna. *Jonas* I say. *Jonas* says Rosalie. Leave me now I say. And again. Are there three sisters? Yes, there are three. I associate only with the three Jouet sisters any more. *Rabble* I say to enrage them. *Rabble* says Anna. *Gangs of thieves. Gangs of thieves* repeats Josepha. *Industry in school, industry in general, industry in particular* I say quickly. *Industry in school, industry in general, industry in particular* says Rosalie. *But not alone* I say. They are silent. *Tent, tent,* I call. Nothing. I bend over my writings again. *Tent*? No, not *tent*, they don't understand anything about that. *Foreign regions* I call out over their heads. *Foreign regions* Rosalie repeats hesitantly, *foreign regions* says Anna. *Foreign regions* says Josepha. Too softly, one almost doesn't hear her. I have to turn to other subjects, maybe to subjects of a fair. Too poor. Or to subjects of the hunt. To leather stools, to English rifles. Or requisites for embroidery? I cannot decide. My pen drips, the Jouet sisters have directed their eyes towards me. I know now there must be school things, notebooks, bindings, the history of West Africa in cardboard covers. But I have no words for it, not a sound. They look at me, these sisters, and I bring nothing in. In this landscape it's a question of what's brought in, one must know that. And one must know it beforehand, before the letters, before all else. Profitable results are the usual thing here. Only then comes the flora then the fauna and whatever else is produced, snake islands, demarcations of boundary, most is to be negotiated, to be well accommodated under cabin roofs. I saw a flock of cranes in formation held firm in flight, stuffed with feathers, nailed on wooden stands. In the correct arrangement, that was not easy. A beautiful flock. Rosalie would say that too. If she desired to say it. Rosalie is blond. She has thin hair and wears it parted like her grandmother in the motherland. What am I

saying? We won't speak about it, I'll hold to that, it won't be too
hard for me. Anna and Josepha don't remember it any longer, they
are dark and look straight ahead. When they speak to me they
place themselves right in front of me; Rosalie doesn't have to do
that. She grazes my shoulder, she speaks from the roof, from the
dirty monuments, and out from behind the corn barrels. The
motherland, that's a laugh, we'll leave that now. When Rosalie
goes out into the desert the border guards take notice under their
burnooses but they don't dare say anything. Rosalie goes often
into the desert. I could imagine sand for my writings. She drags
it here in a Chinese child's dipper. The sand is her pretext, her
reason for me. For her herself her desert walks will have different
reasons, her own reasons. She collects nut shells, says Josepha and
looks rigidly at me, always from the front. She keeps the desert in
order. She gives drawing lessons, calls Anna, she took me along
twice. She taught me the swan and the duck. The species says
Josepha. Naturally the species Anna replies, absent-minded. With
hook shoes, black patent from home. Home, home? My country.
It cracked when we came home. I mean when we came here, each
time the two times, it crunched in our stockings, yes, it did that.
We'll take that gladly upon ourselves, says Josepha, won't we
Rosalie? *Upon ourselves* I say. *Upon ourselves*, that suits me, I'll
take that. *Upon ourselves*. Well what do you think? says Rosalie.
That's the way she is. A desert teacher. And then web-footed birds.
With the collected nut shells as fins. *Fin school* I call, *fin school* I
call now and clap my hands. I know I have no inkling about
nursery schools, but I should have, I should feel myself as a dream
and should stick to cleanliness, that would correspond to the
whole. *The sand out of the shoes* I would have to call, and after a
suitable minute *hand your teacher the salt, Josepha*. Or *Anna*. Or
Anna too. But I don't do it. I take my Jouet sisters as they are, in-
clined towards beggar women at the edge of the desert, often
without charm. As a branch, as a dried out hurricane, as a darling.
Or darlings. As company. With three gradations. We never go
fishing with each other. No game preserve. Nothing but my ex-
aggerations hold us together. I may not therefore give them up, I
must hold on to my table and continue to write my reports, about
the country to the motherland, about the motherland to the coun-
try. In between *naufrage*. They are the threads. *The bricks sink in
here*, it says in one of my reports, I came upon that by myself. *The
straw flies away from it there*, it says in the next one, I simply
believe that. I saw it fly with my eyes closed. There were travellers
too who told me about it. *They don't believe how the straw flies
there*, they related and kept going. *Especially on the west coast*. My

pen scratches, it is my first pen. Don't exaggerate says Rosalie. Don't exaggerate, Anna says also. It is your second. Isn't it? Oh, yes. Your second, says Josepha soothingly and her gray dress rustles, your second pen. Naturally. Shortly thereafter I see her cowering at my table leg picking lint. When we escaped the cannibals, you broke the first one. I know, I know. Your second peace. My second peace, who says that? Josepha said it. Josepha? It is my third peace Josepha. *Poor Jonas*, Josepha says gently. That is surprising. Since I was washed ashore no one has said it. No one represents him as poor, who must make do with his eating utensils. Or with shoulders, with the sense of smell. Poor Samson, you have only one nose, it would have to read, but it doesn't go that way. I had a place-setting with me besides. In the bread sack it was complete. Josepha polished it from time to time, she sits down in the temple porch and rubs at it. In her indication of a junk. During this a compote spoon got lost, maybe that's what she meant. For the rest it sparkles more strongly than in childhood days at the rivers, stronger than ever before. And I seldom eat compote, the water here is brackish, many kinds of fruits are destroyed in it with their sugar. One can also get by with cattle, with lion eyes, and a hint of dill over it. Rosalie laughs. She collected the dill. With her sister Anna, there was none. We all ate from it. *Serve yourself*, sir, the three said *go ahead and have some*. The table was covered brilliantly. All white, a half tropical kind of forget-me-not stuck to each fork, for the preservation of this very variety we are making do with it. Around each setting a silk string from the motherland, about that I should be silent. There are no female spinners here, the white fathers refrain from that. *Rain* says Anna and gets busy on the roof. *Rain* says Rosalie, *rain* says Josepha. Unanimously and it is already streaming from the sky. That could suit you all, yes, that would be just right for you all. Straining to listen, straining to sleep, letting the decoration pour in, my dear sisters, that's the way you would like it, but not I. Why are you called Jouet? Are there zones there where you come from, divine guests in the old manner? Do the fish contain iodine there? What induced your father to each of you? And on the other hand by what was he induced to himself? I am alone without you. I have only you in mind. Why are you so gray, so pink, orange, blue and the rest? So resigned as if you did not know what to do? Or do you think that I am exaggerating again Rosalie? Do you think so Anna? Do you think so Josepha? Do I exaggerate? Am I rash, frivolous? Is that what one calls that? I should say *rain* and let it patter. Cover shrubbery, mission schools, beacon light in the mud, everything is symmetrically undermined. I should say *rain* after you and breathe in the dampness greedily like your paternal relatives, as soon as they had a presentiment of the dining tables painted longitudinally, a long time before you all. As soon as their automatic water pipes went out in the forecourts which was soon. Someone by the name Boats has said currently, inventively, opaquely that he knows it, a cousin of your great uncle, he did not take after you. Leave him, he likes to loll about at fires. These old additions, what should one do with them? One tramples them down and they age again right away. Fire, with fires, hanging with white, soil-scarred, yes. Legitimately, there we would be again. With both feet on the beds of the rivers which bear generals' names, on the breeding grounds for hook-worms, everything already sketched in, I know, I'll stop now too. I bow to my sisters who are gray and white. Who has no legs and can walk anyway, can tear out the traps for the desert foxes, who is that? That is you three, my loves. The Jouets were pleasant, it will be said of you, they were all three very pleasant, thus it is said, is that all right with you? They had church plantings where no one expected it, near Schaffhausen for example, they drank the water away from the drowning people. One could play six-handed well with them. What did it say again? They were devoted it said. Now you know it. The salvaged desert foxes are digging you into the light. Devoted, what do you say to that? Surrounded one who well could have been their father. Devoted. I say nothing to that, I am waiting, for what you say, I am waiting for nothing else. What you say, I say. What do you say? *School building*? Very good. *School building* says Rosalie, *school building* Anna, *school building* says Josepha. *Josepha's house* says Rosalie. With *windows*. What will come next? Table and uniform, velar or labial, secret, seal-hunting? I am waiting, I am waiting. For monkey-bread and peanut, pad of cotton-wool, pastry, and heroes of the fatherland. Ascension into heaven and the command that belongs to it. My sweet doves, my wooden lights. How should I say Amen, before you say it?

RADIO PLAY

THE JOUET SISTERS

ROSALIE JOUET
JOSEPHA JOUET
ANNA JOUET

In the open air.

JOSEPHA: What did Rosalie say?

ANNA: Earth.

JOSEPHA: That was careless of her.

ANNA: What do you mean?

JOSEPHA: I mean, she hardly says it before it stacks up in piles, lies around in strips, in mountains, hummocks, waves. Whatever you like.

ANNA: Do stop it.

JOSEPHA: A new one has started up there.

ANNA: That is the sun.

JOSEPHA: Is that still there too? Ruins one's view.

ANNA: The one over there is new.

JOSEPHA: I agree with that.

ANNA: A tract of land. *(When Josepha remains silent.)* Natives are already dancing on it.

JOSEPHA: Everything to her credit. Our dear sister.

ANNA: Leave her be.

JOSEPHA: Our dear sister is creating the world for herself. Strips of land, potash works. Even to the point of the flags of the papal ambassador.

ANNA: And? Why shouldn't she?

JOSEPHA: Just a matter of consideration.

ROSALIE *(lively)*: Here I am again. It was beautiful, so cold. The papal ambassador got sick.

ANNA: Do you hear?

ROSALIE: I saw him through the window. I asked him HOW ARE YOU REVEREND? GOOD, GOOD, MY CHILD. WHAT ARE THE MAGNOLIAS DOING THAT I BROUGHT TO YOU? YOU BROUGHT THEM IS THAT TRUE? THAT IS TRUE.

JOSEPHA: True.

ROSALIE: He said IF THAT IS TRUE THEN I'LL GIVE YOU ONE AND IN ADDITION SOME APPLES.

ANNA: Where are they?

ROSALIE: We digressed.

JOSEPHA *(sharply)*: Where to?

ROSALIE: Early writings.

ANNA: What?

ROSALIE: Sketched-in velar, uvular and labial sounds. A passion of his. *(Yawning.)* He spoke for a long time.

JOSEPHA: I want to ask you something, Rosa. Did you fabricate the strip of land, east northeast, 220 to 6000?

ROSALIE *(chewing)*: That one is old.

JOSEPHA: Yesterday?

ROSALIE: Yes, maybe yesterday. I didn't think anything would come of it. Is it growing?

ANNA: They are already staking it out.

ROSALIE: What do they want to plant?

ANNA: They are dancing on it.

ROSALIE: If the ambassador knew that. He would be there immediately. Would get up from his sick bed, drape himself in cotton. A ma très chère Delphine.

JOSEPHA: Stop fabricating!

ROSALIE: An epitaph, honestly.

JOSEPHA: They are beginnings.

ROSALIE: I am happy when they dance. Heads high and up and down, up and down and on and on do you hear? Maybe I'll go right over.

ANNA *(quickly)*: Stay here, Rosalie, show us! Let us with you — the new world —

ROSALIE: You were there. Twice.

JOSEPHA: Do you mean at the salt brine which dried up again instantly?

ROSALIE: Because you left. And the peanut mountain?

ANNA: A mountain of shells.

ROSALIE: Was that nothing? Shells without nuts and as high as I don't know what, but high. And in addition two girls in colored smocks who were collecting, were looking for nuts.

JOSEPHA: Didn't know that you had made the shells for yourself, with grooves and cracks, and they almost got buried under the mountain. Anna and I pulled them out while a man in a stiff hat turned around the tracks and did not look back. Three times. He must have been from you too.

ANNA: The poor creatures spit, looked pale.

JOSEPHA: And were fed by us, by the trifling tea that we still had.

ROSALIE: By you two, there you have it.

JOSEPHA: And if they had not gone away, your two? If we had had no tea for them? No bandages for the scratches on the fingers?

ROSALIE: Questions, questions.

ANNA: But they ran away immediately, refreshed and strengthened with bandages, so fast and so happily. Yes, happily! You can't call it anything else.

ROSALIE: Go ahead and call it that.

ANNA: The man with the hat turned again around the tracks symmetrically like before.

JOSEPHA: I tell you, stop fabricating, Rosa!

ANNA: But it didn't disturb me. You see, Josepha, I called, if it hadn't been for us!

JOSEPHA: And then you called: They are our joys!

ROSALIE *(laughs)*: Poor Josepha!

JOSEPHA: The shell mountain towered before us and we only had the choice: were we supposed to wait until you fabricated the next one who would have the desire to eat at it until he was satisfied. Or not.

ROSALIE: I did not fabricate anyone else. The one who kept turning around the tracks was the father. That was enough for me.

JOSEPHA: Since then you have fabricated 62 new ones.

ROSALIE: With the countries that belong to them. I did that. Should they have no countries or at least chickens? Butterflies over their vegetable beds?

Clapping and drums in the distance.

JOSEPHA: That sounds different.

ROSALIE: Straw sacks, sagas of the stars, readers from the motherland?

JOSEPHA: Stop it now!

ANNA: Yes, don't make her angry, Rosa.

ROSALIE: My last eleven are quite lively.

JOSEPHA: And then to bring the motherland into it. You. The motherland.

115

ROSALIE: This old desert. Impossible to fabricate.

JOSEPHA (*almost crying*): Do you hear, Anna? Make a note of all that, keep it in mind!

ROSALIE: You can do nothing more with it either.

ANNA: I still remember. Sweet springs.

ROSALIE: Yes, yes!

ANNA: Horse races, the crack when the clay doves broke, the laughter of the young recruits.

ROSALIE: I don't fabricate those things.

JOSEPHA: And your dancers over there? Your little cannibals with their salt eyes?

ROSALIE: Mine?

JOSEPHA: And the rolled up flags, the lukewarm storms in the embassy quarter, your envoy with his cold.

ROSALIE: The good man.

JOSEPHA: The fishwives who laughed about the burst guts of the morays.

ROSALIE (*crossly*): That did happen.

ANNA: The liver is supposed to be poisonous.

JOSEPHA: Go ahead and find reasons for her, let her continue to fabricate! Junks, entrance hallways, new nations.

ROSALIE: I fabricated only those fishwives who remained serious. I mean the one who stood behind them.

JOSEPHA: Perjury already at nine.

ROSALIE: Do you both remember the one with the brown coat? She didn't laugh.

JOSEPHA: I didn't see any that didn't laugh.

ROSALIE: Who had only the coat on, do you mean that one?

JOSEPHA: And lifted if up and wiped her mouth with it?

ROSALIE: She didn't laugh.

JOSEPHA: Because she was yours? Did you fabricate the flat face at the same time? And who knows why she didn't laugh? And why shouldn't she have laughed?

ROSALIE: Yes, why not?

ANNA (*eagerly*): I'd know that.

JOSEPHA: You, you! You want to support Rosalie, you've admired her for a long time. Stare at her eagerly when she leans on the graves of her dark colonels and concocts new fabrications.

ANNA: But I know it Josepha, the woman remained serious. I

116

turned around when you asked what it was and pointed to the swollen fish. She didn't contort her face. She also has a little boy in the Baptist kindergarten. In the lower section.

JOSEPHA: A little boy with the Baptists?

ANNA: I know her.

JOSEPHA: When did you fabricate him, Rosalie?

ROSALIE: At the same time I did her, shortly after the period of rain. I think it was a Wednesday. He is pretty.

ANNA: She picks him up every day. Always at five.

JOSEPHA: And what did you expect of him when you made him up?

ROSALIE *(surprised)*: Me? Nothing. It is possible that he has a weak character too.

ANNA: I don't believe that.

JOSEPHA: Anna knows. Again Anna knows.

ANNA: The way he holds his mother's hand and walks along beside the cafés.

ROSALIE: He has bad eyes. Short-sighted I believe.

JOSEPHA: Then make up glasses for him.

ROSALIE: No.

JOSEPHA: One word.

ANNA: Or fabricate broad shoulders for him, strong arms, a justifiable pride! A beautiful two-colored shirt?

ROSALIE: I tried that.

JOSEPHA: Do you hear? Tried. Tried a little boy for the Baptist kindergarten. She doesn't know what will come of it, but she is trying it anyway. That's really something. Has no notion of the great laws but she tries it.

ROSALIE: I ask myself often too: Will eggs agree with him? And all that.

ANNA: Does he know you?

ROSALIE: It's not impossible.

ANNA: And did you make up the Baptist kindergarten too, Rosie?

ROSALIE: Didn't you know it? It was already there.

JOSEPHA: Like many other things. But it could be from you with its glaring appearance. With its lower and its upper sections.

ROSALIE: Yes, what all might not be from me. But you are right, it could be from me. A couple of curls less at the gutter, some pails of sand more for the lower and the upper sections —

JOSEPHA: Be careful, Rosa!

ROSALIE: And he would be an object of my pride, but I'll leave it. I don't like to repeat myself either.

JOSEPHA: Repeat!

ROSALIE: He has similarities with the little giraffe to which I gave life in March. The flaky appearance, the ravenous hunger.

JOSEPHA: The sections. I should have known right away that it was from you.

ANNA: It came out successfully for her, Josepha!

JOSEPHA: Successfully? Not one morning did it not smell at our thorn-bush, sniff at our bed and rub its neck on our camel-hair blanket. The terror of all expeditions since.

ANNA: I am happy whenever I see it.

JOSEPHA: The most annoying and monstrous giraffe of my stay here, does it have companions?

ROSALIE: Not yet. But I am thinking about it.

JOSEPHA: Its neck is too short.

ROSALIE: Intentionally.

ANNA: Does it eat haws of plants, Rosie?

ROSALIE: Yes, haws.

ANNA: Then it's the one.

JOSEPHA: And the haws? You simply take. You don't even make the effort to fabricate them if I know you.

ROSALIE: It is effort enough for it to eat them.

JOSEPHA: You simply use the lovely things which are there?

ROSALIE: They scratch their necks, I should have taken violets, or jasmine, I mean the local one. But it doesn't complain.

JOSEPHA: There it comes.

ANNA: How it is jumping. Before its legs are above the horizon I recognize it.

ROSALIE: It is trying to get to the dancers.

ANNA: They aren't dancing any more.

ROSALIE: I see that.

ANNA: Won't they try to kill it? Won't they chase it, Rosie?

ROSALIE: When I fabricated it I whispered to them that giraffe meat is tough and harmful and that the hide is ugly.

ANNA: I wonder if they believe you?

ROSALIE: It looks as if they were deliberating. One has climbed up on a rock. Tall Samson!

JOSEPHA: Names.

ANNA *(curious)*: Where do you get them?

ROSALIE: They are standing around. In the sand, on linen sacks, on the monuments. I just take my choice.

JOSEPHA: He has a powerful voice, your Samson.

ANNA: What is he saying? *(When Rosalie doesn't answer.)* Tell us, Rosa!

ROSALIE: He is calling my giraffe, he calls it the composite animal, he asks it how it had successfully vaulted over the edge of the desert.

ANNA: And what does it say?

JOSEPHA: It explains it to him. *(Listening.)* With the help of its neck, its legs, skeleton. Very good.

ANNA: It scratches miserably.

ROSALIE: With the help of the desert edge itself which served as a support for it. That was the best thing.

JOSEPHA: It was weak.

ROSALIE: Oh, yes, Josepha.

ANNA: They are now still.

JOSEPHA: That makes little difference to us.

ROSALIE *(calmly)*: What do you want?

JOSEPHA: I defend myself. I am not Anna who waits patiently for you to conjure up more cannibals, cisterns that make us thirsty, ambassadors with colds. Or until an early afternoon fabricated by you, acquires the desire for my last joys. I don't want to know your secret either, your tricks, I should say, I don't want to have anything to do with minor leaders who have died off and who found it necessary to become colonels. And not for all of heaven itself would I like to have invented this ridiculous animal over there, your Samson with his tree stumps or the nameless boy for the Baptist kindergarten.

ROSALIE: His name is Bergson.

JOSEPHA: That is not so.

ROSALIE: He will be happy.

JOSEPHA: He will be happy. Whether he gets the first handful of sand in his face or the last adulation which kills him, he will be happy. Whether scarlet fever or itch, mouth disease or enlistment orders of his tireless fatherlands — he will be happy. He will always say MY NAME IS BERGSON.

ANNA: It is true, Rosie, don't you want to give him some more usual name? Osseynou or Jean? Recently I read that Papa David would be good too, Sabine was possible not long ago as a masculine name for first-born children. Everything possible.

ROSALIE: His name is Bergson. *(In various pitches of voice.)* Bergson, Bergson.

ANNA: A name is like a nose. I am in favor of second names.

ROSALIE: Bergson Paul.

ANNA: Bergson Paul!

ROSALIE: We'll call him Bergson Paul. The little Bergson Paul. Terrible.

ANNA: You see, one can reason with her, Josepha. Amicably.

ROSALIE: Good Anna. But he will undertake it for you. Bergson Paul. At the first itch he will not even notice it. And with the last one he will have gotten used to it. I will tell him, for Anna, when he starts to complain, for Anna. You can do it for Anna. When he goes ashore in Cannes, swinging along, a sailor, Bergson Paul —

JOSEPHA: Where will you put him ashore?

ROSALIE: It will sound in his ears always. For ANNA!

ANNA: Cannes, where is that?

ROSALIE: Until then it's there.

JOSEPHA: Rosalie has already had more success.

ROSALIE: In the Antilles or on the contrary. It will have its difficulties, but you are correct, Josepha: I shall succeed.

JOSEPHA: No doubt.

ROSALIE: Three years ago I was most successful with a New Year's greeting. At that time I knew nothing about Bergson Paul.

ANNA: I wish you luck for Cannes, Rosa, that it will be beautiful! With coats of arms, switchboards and with even more things of life.

ROSALIE: Perhaps I'll take stony beaches upon myself, some tar, naval hospitals like everywhere, it won't disturb Bergson. You are right, Anna, wish us happiness!

JOSEPHA: Yes, wish her happiness, wish her only happiness! I have an idea it will be a station for cannibals, one of the many to whom Rosalie has lent her power of fabrication. And will still lend as long as we permit it. With coats of arms, switchboards, perhaps even a peacock feather at the gangway. Or should it be an ordinary rooster that must believe in you?

ANNA: As long as we permit it? What are you saying Josepha? *(Shocked, altered.)* What is that?

JOSEPHA: Just as I was saying.

ANNA: She is correct, Rosa, they are coming nearer. They are leading the giraffe in the middle of them, they are threatening us. Rosa, Rosa!

ROSALIE *(calmly)*: They want to ask me something.

JOSEPHA *(angrily)*: Then keep them from it.

ROSALIE: *(clicks with her tongue)*.

JOSEPHA: You are threatening us with your fabrications.

ROSALIE: I stopped them.

ANNA: But they are nearer now. Do you think they will stay there, Rosie? Or that they will strive to go back to their old region?

JOSEPHA *(mimicing Anna)*: Do you think that they will strive to go to the southeast or the southwest, Rosie? Or do you think that they will be shortly with us? Around us, under us? If you asked me, Anna, I could tell you.

ROSALIE: It is their region, they have enlarged it. The thorny but good road. Now they have to stake it off. They will have their work cut out for them.

ANNA: I wonder if it might not be better to pack the baskets and return to town? It was a fine picnic and also instructive, I am again and again in favor of the southern edge of the desert. One can sit here better even if it gets damp towards evening, the thorn-bushes give more shade here than in the north, one prefers in the end to go home. You'll see Bergson again. If we leave now we'll be at the Baptist kindergarten right at five. *(Taking a breath.)* It was good that we took the afternoon.

JOSEPHA: It would be good for us now if we were afraid. Afraid, afraid, afraid enough and even more afraid of our sister, of her plans. Who started with this picnic? Who mentioned it as casually as possible when we were standing in the bookstore, when I intended to return the bad edition of Rosetti?

ROSALIE: Four pages misprinted, with the exception of the translation.

JOSEPHA: Who began to run in order that we would get all provisions in time, who rented the car, chose the driver and as long as we were still undecided, kept bringing into the conversation the cool breath of air which today distinguishes the edge of the desert?

ROSALIE: The southern edge.

ANNA: I did too, Josepha, remember! I said it too. Are we here for the first time? Doesn't each of us have a favorite branch on this thorn-bush for hat and coat?

JOSEPHA: I no longer. Since my coat became tattered and the vultures got my blue straw hat. And that was a long time ago.

ANNA: Rosalie bought you a new one.

ROSALIE: The old one was worth nothing. Too round for your head.

ANNA: Don't provoke her Rosa! And don't either of you laugh, I beg, don't laugh like you're doing now! One shouldn't laugh in anger. Do you want my cloth Josepha?

JOSEPHA (muffled): No.

ANNA: I love this spot of sand. And you both do too. You know you do.

JOSEPHA: What plans do you have for us Rosa? Do you want to fabricate roperies for ropes at the lower strip of coast? Or weaving mills for silk ribbons which are meant to tie off our necks? Canoes which are unproven for renowned water outings, a nitrogen plant in the east with the west wind requisite to it? With what will you enrich still almighty nature? With alligators which turned out too long, a new epidemic of unknown origin? Do you want to set right a new kind of river whirlpool?

ROSALIE (morosely): Do be quiet.

JOSEPHA: Or is the little group over there enough, staking out their land so carefully? With peeled branches, no, staves, stripped and pointed and long enough to stake out many more countries? Anna is right, it is a good place. At least to find out whence the wind is blowing. (After a minute.) By the way, they have already come nearer again. Act sometimes as if they were deliberating. But they are not deliberating. You can see the patterns cut into the staves.

ANNA: Pretty aren't they, Rosie, Josepha?

JOSEPHA (exhausted): Your sense of beauty, Rosalie. Do we still have some tea?

ANNA: There, go ahead Josepha, strengthen yourself! Look over there how beautifully Rosie's giraffe has turned out. How everything sparkles.

JOSEPHA: They have tied its legs.

ANNA (horrified): But why Rosalie?

ROSALIE: Heaven knows. (She clicks with her tongue.)

ANNA: Do they hear you?

JOSEPHA: Or are they already managing without you?

ROSALIE (clicks again, then calmly): Now.

ANNA: They are untying it. But it wouldn't have been necessary to scare us so. Are they not light-skinned, Rosa? I thought they were colored?

ROSALIE: Faded, uncolored, colorless, without hue, not colored. I'm not sure. Who said something about GIVING A HELPING HAND?

JOSEPHA: Samson is dark.

ANNA: They are going to leave again.

JOSEPHA: Oh never. But I shall leave. I shall need a long night after this picnic. And the morning after won't be particularly good either.

ROSALIE: We palefaces. *(As if imitating a sermon.)* Color has been taken from us because of our sins.

JOSEPHA: I'll not wait either until you two have decided. I'll wait until the tea has given me strength. Then I'll go to temple and I'll take the bus.

ROSALIE: We are coming to a monument. Because of good behavior during, during I don't know what.

ANNA: The car has been ordered, Josepha. I'll be glad to pick it up. It costs the same whether we take it for two or for three people.

JOSEPHA: Then take it for you two.

ROSALIE: Left, right, down below. Over that the relief of another one. If I only knew whose relief.

ANNA: I would also like to go. It was I who first mentioned departure.

JOSEPHA: You will never drive home without Rosalie, Anna. You two are in agreement.

ANNA: I wouldn't know about what.

JOSEPHA: All the worse.

ANNA: Or do you know what we are in agreement about? Rosalie?

JOSEPHA: *(laughs)*.

ROSALIE: Sometimes I see myself as a charcoal grate for something that is still to be roasted. A half goat, a calf. Or as a spit. *(She clicks with her tongue.)* Again. I don't know what pleasure it is to tie up someone's legs. Tightly over the hips.

JOSEPHA *(sharply)*: Watch out, Rosa.

ROSALIE: I am watching out.

ANNA: Does anyone want more tea or should I close the bottle?

ROSALIE: I don't want anything.

JOSEPHA: Rosalie doesn't need anything. She fabricates taking tea without the troublesome detour by way of the lips.

ROSALIE: Especially chicken and ham. Without the troublesome detour by way of chicken and ham. And white bread. I hate talk about cultivation. Undulating fields.

JOSEPHA: And those over there? Should they establish a planting, perhaps according to the model of 1876? Tilling the soil? A village, a fireplace? Or do you only let them stake off their land and let it disappear like the undulating fields of January? I am going now to temple and I am taking the bus.

ROSALIE: This talk!

The rustling of clothes.

ANNA *(hesitantly)*: I have to agree with Josepha, Rosie.

ROSALIE: It looks like flight.

JOSEPHA: Where is my shawl? And who will take the blankets?

ROSALIE: Strike the tent etcetera? Collect your forgotten tea-spoons, sugar and salt tins?

JOSEPHA: I'll leave that to your talent for fabrication. *(Raging.)* To your fairy favor. Undertake a trip with our car, have fun. Fabricate a second in addition, other dimensions, three quarters, one and a half times bigger than our size.

ROSALIE *(chewing)*: Mmm.

JOSEPHA: Suitable for your Samson.

ROSALIE: Or for Bergson and his mother.

JOSEPHA: As you like.

ROSALIE: Your dress is torn.

JOSEPHA: *(shaken by a fit of coughing)*.

ROSALIE: Should I invent a patch over it?

JOSEPHA *(still coughing)*: No.

ROSALIE: I would be in favor of it.

JOSEPHA *(exasperated)*: I believe that. *(Already at a distance.)* But bear in mind one thing, Rosalie. I prefer everything without your fabrications. The way it is. Even the bubonic plague.

ROSALIE: There she goes.

ANNA: She forgot her money. Josepha!

ROSALIE: I'll fabricate it inside her pocket.

ANNA: Josepha!

ROSALIE: While you have forgotten again to accompany her. I would like to know how she gets into the bus with her trailing dress, surrounded by helpers. *(Imitating Josepha.)* Thank you very much, thank you from the bottom of my heart, but it

124

wouldn't have been necessary, Mr. Clermont, are you going the same way?

ANNA: It could well be. This Clermont from the book store goes to temple often towards evening. He takes the bus back.

ROSALIE: It will not be pleasant for her if he sees the rip in her dress.

ANNA: He will help her.

ROSALIE: THE UNTIDY SISTERS he will think. HOW FAR THEY'VE SUNK.

ANNA: He won't think that.

ROSALIE: THESE DWARF BUSTARDS ARE DRIVING ALONG THE DESERT EDGE WITH RAGGED COATS. WHEN I THINK WHAT RESPECTABLE GRANDFATHERS THEY HAD.

ANNA: He doesn't know that.

ROSALIE: But he will think it. AND EVEN IF THERE WAS SOME FAULT TO BE FOUND IN THE GRANDFATHERS THE GREAT UNCLES WERE AFTER ALL FIRST CLASS. JACOB FOR INSTANCE FROM AUVERGNE, AND EDUARD FROM HESSE. WITH THE EXCEPTION OF SOLOMON WHO SMOKED HIS PIPE ON THE LEFT SIDE, WITH THE LOMBARDY RELATIONSHIP AND THE ROYAL FAMILIES IN THE BACKGROUND. ONE SHOULD NOT SWITCH THE CONTINENT, IT ENDS WITH THE GREAT NIECES. WHAT COULD THEY BE DOING AT HOME BESIDE THE BLOOMING RIVERS? AND HERE? THEY ARE STUFFING OATS IN THEIR SHOES; OR BEDFEATHERS.

ANNA: Oats and bedfeathers are the best during the rainy season, how are you to dry out your shoes otherwise? And since when are we so bad off, since when can't we take the morning paper any more and stuff into our shoes as soon as they are damp? Since when have we been lolling around at walls or standing on windy corners considering which car we should take, which driver for which picnic which we cannot legitimately afford any longer?

ROSALIE: Yes, yes.

ANNA: I beg you stop fabricating, Rosie!

ROSALIE: Now the bus is moving. And Mr. Clermont is probably sitting next to Josepha.

ANNA: Listen to me, Rosalie!

ROSALIE: Listen, stop, I shall fabricate new words for you.

ANNA *(crying)*: No, no!

ROSALIE: Then I won't.

ANNA: How nice it was when we still had our stand at the craft fair. When Josepha then after her activity waited for us down below at the fence and we discussed the inn for the evening. When we arranged the freshly arrived goods in the morning.

ROSALIE: I was fabricating already at that time.

ANNA *(tearfully)*: What?

ROSALIE: Here and there a better arrangement for the rings, a customer, who did not steal. Or only one more stone before my feet, a booth with woolen house shoes, before which they gathered.

ANNA: Was that necessary, Rosa?

ROSALIE: So our stand was always protected from the sun. Josepha noticed nothing, she was waiting outside. And our little Anna also noticed nothing.

ANNA: I would rather have endured the sun.

ROSALIE: I would rather endure nothing. Intentionally. Only because Josepha made me angry with her talk from the embassy quarter — eating more quietly, using nicer language, living with pleasure — I made up the papal embassy.

ANNA *(blowing her nose)*: There are now two. They are already talking about them. And why did you give your ambassador the chronic cold which ties him to the bed and you act as if he had caught a new cold every day?

ROSALIE *(chewing)*: Stupid, but he was supposed to be different from the others. I also like to talk to him through the open window.

ANNA: I still don't understand you, Rosie. Because Josepha was bragging, because the sun was shining. Are they your reasons?

ROSALIE: Yes.

ANNA: Are they enough to justify plunging us into misfortune? To register us with the reputation of peculiarity? What does one think of someone who fabricates papal embassies? Or John Donne editions which were never published?

ROSALIE: We shall find that out, dear Anna.

ANNA: I was always on your side, Rosalie.

ROSALIE: Since Josepha left you are on your own side.

ANNA: You are heartless, Rosie. What was that?

ROSALIE: The giraffe screamed again. That's now the third time. Another attempt to tie its legs and I shall dissolve them over there.

ANNA: Do it, Rosie. Like that time the field along the fishing

126

shore, it didn't suit, and you made it disappear again. After only seven minutes.

ROSALIE: Too quickly.

ANNA: You listened to us and acknowledged our arguments.

ROSALIE: This time I'll have to be more careful.

ANNA: Don't wait too long to think about it. Leave the giraffe if you like it but not the others. Not this giant with his hoe. *(Frightened.)* They have come closer again, Rosalie. You know it.

ROSALIE: Know, know, know.

ANNA: Then you'll see it.

ROSALIE: That is also such a thing.

ANNA: They will threaten us. They will try to tie our legs as well as those of your giraffe.

ROSALIE: Perhaps I'll have Bergson come then. Or the one with the hat, who never stops going around the corner. A cage, a peanut mountain.

ANNA: Don't overestimate yourself.

ROSALIE: No. If need be I can displace the second papal embassy. Over the entire thing. *(Calls.)* Samson stop! *(After a moment.)* I did him an injustice. I thought he intended now to kill the giraffe, but he only wants to hoe the soil. That's all right. *(Thoughtfully.)* Cultivator of the soil and cattle-breeder.

ANNA *(simply)*: That would be all right too.

ROSALIE: It is inconceivable. *(To herself.)* Moon, moon — butter, butter — cobbler, cobbler — rime, rime.

ANNA: Rosalie.

ROSALIE *(more rapidly)*: Bride, bride — Josef, Josef — gray, gray — *(catching her breath)* dipper, dipper — region, region —

ANNA: End, End!

ROSALIE: Thus one can name it too. *(Exhausted.)* I thought perhaps a breath would be inserted between the old names and tear them to pieces in the end. But even the images from the air still conform to them. Even my Samson. *(Mocking.)* I think they are beginning now to plant turnips. But I shall invent a volcano for them if they should thrive, their own rain of ashes which covers them and retains their forms for posterity.

ANNA: To what are you being driven, Rosie? If you turn over all of your fabrications to volcanoes? Wouldn't it be better to let them disappear before they come to, before they have entirely lost their ethereal substance? First Samson or Bergson? The papal ambassador or the giraffe? Begin, Rosalie, begin, let them go! There is a papal ambassador in our town, why have a second one? There are sailors that go ashore somewhere, more than enough, why Bergson? There are giraffes in this country, why yours with the short back? False proportions, Josepha is right there. Not to mention the mountain of peanut shells and the two girls.

ROSALIE: They were experiments.

ANNA: And as such we have looked at them. But you are perfecting yourself each day, you are getting better and better, Rosie, and that is dangerous for us all. Your Samson has a fine shape.

ROSALIE: Yes?

ANNA: Muscle movement, better proportions, somewhat too large but otherwise he is perfect. When he is no longer made of air he'll kill us. With his turnip hoe which then will no longer be made of air either. Or with a fishing line, an English rifle, a cowhide horsewhip. Whatever has occurred to you up till then for him.

ROSALIE: Nothing more will occur to me for him.

ANNA: His bare hands are sufficient too.

ROSALIE: You are good, Annie, you are also getting better and better. With the progressing half hours or what does one call it? Do you see how astonished my people are over there about the cranes taking flight? I believe I will have to teach them the feathered world, aerial tricks, sense of direction, chicken eggs, the eggs themselves. It could happen otherwise that Samson gets one on his head and the yoke runs down over his eyes useless. They are ignorant. Samson!

ANNA (carefully): He doesn't hear you.

ROSALIE: Akabu, Tyalides, Midas, Gregorovius! How should I begin, Anna? How should I introduce the world of birds? NO PESSIMISTIC OUTLOOK ON LIFE, MY LITTLE ONES. Is that correct?

ANNA: I love birds.

ROSALIE: But how to proceed further? CROWN PRINCE RUDOLF WAS ALREADY SAYING THAT HE HAD KILLED NO KITES AT KORNEUBURG AND ISAAC BABITT EXPLAINED IN YALE THAT ONE MUST NOT BE CARRIED AWAY BY SORROW OVER THE BUSINESS OF BROOD CARE.

ANNA: That is not true, I knew Babitt. He did not say that.

ROSALIE: I AM LOST, SIR, SAID THE GREEN PLOVER IN THE FAIRY

TALE. Would that do? Or should I say it differently? THE LACKING TAMABILITY OF THE SNAKE-HAWK REMAINS FOREVER UNWORTHY OF THE MASTER OF HUNTING RIGHTS. So. That gives a more general picture, that will suit them. WHILE THE STORMY PETRELS AGAIN — and right after BABITT WAS ALREADY SAYING —

ANNA: Leave Babitt out. Begin with the bird calls. It will appease Samson.

ROSALIE: Siksak, kiwit, bibi, djaudjau.

ANNA: Not like that.

ROSALIE: düh dü düll lüllül, achachachachach.

ANNA *(enthusiastically)*: Or with the names of the ornithologists as they called each other from one end of the savannah to the other.

ROSALIE: Jerdon, Adams, Azara, Temminck, is it you, Marquis or the good von Heuglin? Babitt would remain out of it anyway. Huddlestone, Hume, Baldamus, Kalberstein — I know what you would like Anna! Samson to throw away his hoe and to be sung to sleep by this lullabye and to return to the air from which he came with neck and brain and stomach and everything else. Admit it!

ANNA: If I had enough pride I would have been in the next bus a long time, in the next temple, under the next thorn-bush, not next to you.

ROSALIE: I'll start differently too. MY PEOPLE, MY COUNTRY — PEOPLE — *(Softly.)* MY DISTRICT PEOPLE! MY CELEBRITIES, MY SUPERIORS, MY KINGS. I WISH TO TEACH YOU ORNITHOLOGY. WHAT YOU JUST SAW WAS ONLY A FLOCK OF CRANES, IT WAS . MOVING NORTH, is that right, Annie? RIGHT. BUT DON'T EXPECT IT TO REMAIN THUS. THE OIL COLORED EGGS WILL FLY AT YOUR HEADS, THE HOODED AND COWLED VULTURES WILL DARKEN THE SUN, THE SILENT GULLS WILL MAKE TROUBLE FOR YOU, THE GREEN BEAKED ALBATROSSES. FLIGHT, STOPOVER, ESSENCE, YOU WILL HAVE NOTHING OF THEM. STATION, ASTONISHMENT, INSIGHT, A COUPLE OF FEATHERS FOR ADORNMENT, SOME TENDER MORSELS AND IT IS ALL GONE. BABITT, THE GUILLEMOTS, LITTLE KING OTTOCAR, WHO IS SCREAMING IN THE BULRUSHES. AND EVEN IF I LEFT OUT THE SHOEBILLS, THE SEVENTH AND THE TWELFTH CLASSI-FICATION, THERE WOULD BE TOO MUCH THAT WOULD DISAPPEAR. IF I WERE LUCKY AND HAD HIGHER HOOKS I WOULD DRAW THE WORLD OF BIRDS FOR YOU IN THE SAND

BUT MY SISTER JOSEPHA PERSUADED ME TO STRONGER SHOES AND ANNA —

ANNA *(sobbing)*: Let me go!

ROSALIE: A DUCK MIGHT BE CONSIDERED ANYWAY? PERHAPS A MAGPIE. BUT ALREADY THE DRAWING OF THE WINGS OF THE GRAY GOOSE SETS UP THE GREATEST HINDRANCES TO FLAT LANDINGS AND TO A SAND CHANGING INTO EARTH. YOU MUST KNOW THAT, IT BELONGS IN THERE. *(Taking a breath.)* AND WITH THAT I'LL STOP. Do you hear the bells? Bergson's kindergarten is over. Now the moment is coming again when the Baptists are amazed. Towards six then the Unitarians are surprised, at nine the employees of the bank and at three in the morning the military authorities. There is a certain proportion in it but it is not steady.

ANNA: Oh. *(A kind of angry sigh.)*

ROSALIE: But such a strong peal of bells, all to honor my Bergson.

ANNA: Today is by chance the day of unification of our motherland, of its victory over the oppressors on the day of Saint Norman.

ROSALIE: Now they are at the market and are feeding the kites, I hope that his mother picked him up on time. I must begin with Cannes soon, otherwise he'll have no place at which to land. Bergson is growing.

ANNA *(angrily)*: Bergson is growing.

ROSALIE: And I am happy that I fabricated a mother for him whom the guts of rotting morays do not induce to laughter. She has a tendency towards unpunctuality but she will take good care of him. Perhaps she'll open a little hair salon later in Cannes. And my young mate will stop by her place, but she won't clip him smooth. You know, mother, I don't want to be like the recruits. Good, good, good! Farewell, Bergson.

ANNA: Are you crying?

ROSALIE: No.

ANNA: You took good care of him.

ROSALIE: Maybe I'll fabricate a father for him yet, when he is forty.

ANNA: Would you like another sandwich or should I shut the basket?

ROSALIE: I don't know, Anna.

ANNA: There are still apples and sardines. And an egg.

ROSALIE *(exhausted)*: Eggs. No, nothing.

130

ANNA: Don't go to sleep, Rosa. What shall I do here with the baskets, the tent not yet dismantled? There is also still a salmon sandwich, you hear? I'll pack everything and we'll have a splendid evening at home with the remaining tea, a conciliatory celebration with Josepha. Rosa, Rosalie! Will you hand me the half lemon? It lies nearer you.

ROSALIE: My ambassador has died.

ANNA *(after a short silence)*: I am sorry, Rosie. I didn't know him but I liked him, he was perhaps the more agreeable of your fabrications.

ROSALIE: He sat too long at the window. My fault, the house was built too hastily too. A draughty chalet. And in addition presumably the disfavor of the diplomatic corps, of the Tuscan colony, of the Spanish clique etcetera.

ANNA: I can well imagine.

ROSALIE *(bursting out)*: Yes, you both can well imagine. That's as far as it goes. Two thousand throat-rattling edible fish are easy for you to imagine. But a second ambassador with a mild cold unimaginable after all.

ANNA: You are getting confused. It is getting dark too.

ROSALIE: It is getting miserably dark. The motherlands are making themselves noticeable. And our sister Josepha. Is sitting between her straw walls, fresh from the auto with a cup of tea and fabricates counter to it. Bringing my day into the spotlight. Quite simple. I am curious what else will occur to her. Apparently she talked too much about John Donne in the bus with this — what's his name? — Clermont. Our sister accustoms herself however. This future wife of an adjutant, this partner in conversation, this eternal partner who can imagine nothing, nothing, nothing! For whom chickens are parts of children's verses and ducks — rubbish *(More calmly.)* I'll continue to instruct now.

ANNA: In this light?

ROSALIE: I want to call it by its name. These violet bandelets, bandelets of pregnancy, violet, yes, I know. I WANT TO TELL YOU SOMETHING, MY DEARS!

ANNA: Samson is bending. What's happening to them, Rosa?

ROSALIE: Don't interrupt me. I WANT TO TELL YOU SOMETHING. YOU WILL NOT BE NEEDED. AND THAT IS TRUE.

ANNA: Ask him if it is perhaps the appendix.

ROSALIE: IS IT THE APPENDIX, SAMSON?

ANNA: What does he say?

ROSALIE: Nothing.

ANNA: Do you hear?

ROSALIE: The bus clattering inland?

ANNA: They bought it from the third cavalry squadron since it converted in March again to mules.

ROSALIE: I know. For at least the second time. And I know now also what Josepha is: an equestrian statue. Maybe she is lying in bed. I mean in hers, while Clermont lies in his.

ANNA: He is coming nearer again! With the whole entourage behind him. The giraffe is acting also as if it belonged to him. And the violet stripes appear as if they were stuck to its back. Swords, steel blades which it will never be rid of.

ROSALIE: Take a photo!

ANNA *(crying)*: Never again.

ROSALIE *(calmly)*: Not bad. Tell our sister. Tell her she learned the trade. And quickly. Tell her quickly too. Tell her I would never have had the idea of beginning with clearing away. But it is an idea. And tell her she should produce the sea again.

ANNA: And the violet stripes on Samson's back?

ROSALIE: She can leave them. They are good.

ANNA: You are sending me away, Rosa.

ROSALIE: I am sending you into town.

ANNA: You are leaving me in the lurch.

ROSALIE: Run to Josepha!

ANNA: And if I don't find her?

ROSALIE: Then wait for her. But quickly.

ANNA *(already at a distance)*: The temple is gone.

ROSALIE: Take the bus.

ANNA: Should we prepare tea?

ROSALIE: Take it, take it!

ANNA: You both have abandoned me.

ROSALIE: Yes, Anna. No, Anna.

ANNA *(farther away)*: Rosalie!

ROSALIE: What?

ANNA: Your giraffe is beginning to trot.

ROSALIE: I like it when you make jokes, Annie.

ANNA: Yes.

ROSALIE: Hurry!

ANNA: Yes.

ROSALIE: Adieu.

ANNA: Yes.

ROSALIE: She will win yet. Our sister Anna.

ANNA *(rigid)*: I am a place on a gravestone, I am a cradle, a Charlotte, an unadmitted person. I become no longer as I am, and I become not completely what I am.

ROSALIE: Don't come to your senses, Anna!

ANNA *(without letting herself be interrupted in the same tone of voice)*: Encouraging, good-natured, a proposer of picnics, tea pourer, tent pitcher, hat duster, coat shaker, old friend. But here at the edge of the desert —

ROSALIE: I know what it means to find yourself. I can dissuade you.

ANNA: In a lighting which does not suit the edge of the desert, at a coast without sea, before a removed temple facade and after a bus underway, which perhaps has already left, I make a better appearance than my illumined sisters.

ROSALIE: Josepha is supposed to produce the sea again!

ANNA: My sisters who produce and clear away! Who have learned everything more easily than I, pasting postage stamps and catching whale, with white caps in the foam along the way, enthusiastic, stimulated by the western languages which I never understood, entangled in arguments that meant nothing to me. Here I am more, here I can be polite, bowed like all who do not come along, here I am Anna.

ROSALIE: Anna, Anna!

ANNA: Here I am right.

ROSALIE: Run instead!

ANNA: Yes.

ROSALIE: And don't forget to report everything to Josepha.

ANNA: No.

ROSALIE: That way is right.

ANNA *(confused)*: That way it's right? Yes, that way it's really right.

ROSALIE: *(sharply)*: *I* am telling you that, Anna.

ANNA: Should we then return, Josepha and I? Or should we instead wait for you at home? The celery would have to be cooked yet today, otherwise it will dry out, what do you think?

ROSALIE *(perplexed for a moment)*: Yes, what do I think?

ANNA: We will do it properly. First getting the sea.

ROSALIE: And then the celery. Exactly so.

ANNA: Then I'll run now.

ROSALIE: As if I had lost a friend or what does one say on such occasions? Just stop clanking your violet swords, Samson. Let me think, let me think. *(Pause.)* In fact my giraffe is trotting, my young fabrication is fabricating itself anew, I wonder whether that will suit it. Who will tell me? Stop, Samson, stop staking off your land only towards the front. We still have a moment.

JOSEPHA *(out of breath)*: No bus any more. The entire way from town out here on foot. Can you imagine that?

ROSALIE: I cannot imagine your feet, Josepha.

JOSEPHA: And everything in this ridiculous halflight.

ROSALIE: You have failed in something, my sister. But you were not bad. In much even better than I.

JOSEPHA: How can I produce the sea again?

ROSALIE: Anna is on her way to you with the request for it. But how? We didn't think about that. *(After a pause.)* How did you remove it?

JOSEPHA: I said GO! *(Thoughtfully.)* I had just drunk three cups of tea, anger bore me along.

ROSALIE: Does it still bear you? Then run home! Don't take anything away from it, your anger, protect your feet, let yourself be carried! Drink your tea all up and say COME BACK!

JOSEPHA: Some picture postcards were lying on my table.

ROSALIE: Let them lie.

JOSEPHA: And I say simply COME BACK?

ROSALIE: Yes.

JOSEPHA *(dubiously)*: What all might not come back?

ROSALIE: Your anger is diminishing, Josepha.

JOSEPHA: I am hurrying. The lamp was burning on the night-table.

ROSALIE: Let it burn.

JOSEPHA: What if it has gone out?

ROSALIE: Leave it out.

JOSEPHA: And I say simply —

ROSALIE *(calmly)*: Come back.

JOSEPHA: Woe to you if more comes back than was there to begin with. *(At a distance.)* Or less.

ROSALIE: Don't worry.

JOSEPHA: Woe to you, Rosalie.

ROSALIE: Woe is me. Rosalie, that's right. Rosalie, that much is sure.

JOSEPHA *(farther off)*: Rosalie!

ROSALIE *(calls)*: And repeat it! Repeat it. Take more tea.

JOSEPHA: Which kind?

ROSALIE: Which kind did you have?

JOSEPHA *(very far off, like a call for help)*: From Ceylon.

ROSALIE *(calls again)*: All right. From Ceylon. *(She heaves a sigh, then softly, clearly no longer to anyone.)* And be sure. Be sure. They like that. That suits everyone. Don't pull your head in, raise yourself up tall. Long fingers, a straight neck. They are the goals. I know a prescription for the fingers. You pull on them. But for the neck? That's where sensitivity begins, what's the term for it? Dreaminess. I am beginning to lose my mother tongue, quite clearly. Even the expressions which one uses instead of the one which is there. But as quick as that? Get home all right, Josepha! Don't forget how it goes. It goes COME BACK. COME BACK. You must say that. The lamp as it was, the postcards as they were, and then courage, courage. Or should I write a letter to my sisters, two letters? Yes. Letters. Letters in envelopes. *(Eagerly, as if she were writing the first letter.)* DEAR ANNA! I HOPE THAT YOU HAVE GOTTEN HOME ALL RIGHT. Do I hope that? Yes, I hope that. DEAR ANNA. AND THAT YOU DIDN'T RUN INTO ANY SNAKES ON THE WAY, NO DELAY. *(After brief contemplation.)* THAT YOU GOT TO THE BUS. What else? THAT YOU DIDN'T HAVE TO MAKE CONVERSATION ON IT SINCE YOU DON'T LIKE TO HAVE CONVERSATIONS. THAT YOU DIDN'T SLIP OUT. OR SLIDE OUT, YES. THAT YOU DID NOT MEET THE GENTLEMAN EITHER WHO — I HAVE FORGOTTEN THE NAME — WHO ALWAYS GOES THE SAME ROUTE TOO. WHO LIKES TO CONVERSE. AND THAT SOON THE TEMPLE WILL BE STANDING AGAIN. THE FACADE WHICH YOU KNOW. AND THE SEA WITH EVERYTHING, JOSEPHA IS ALREADY ON THE WAY. IT GOES COME BACK. YOUR. So. That is good. And the other? I'll write that one yet too, I'll write everything yet, it won't be difficult. Even if it is difficult for me. MY DEAR JOSEPHA. Right? Right. Or DEAR JOSEPHA? How did it go? More difficult than I thought. MY DEAR JOSEPHA. That's not the way it went. DEAR JOSEPHA. That's the way it went, but did it go that way? I am asking myself too much, it is against good manners. It borders on interference. There they are flying again, the blue birds, the table-talks in the Elysian fields, these words in their harmony, this savings-bank that never relinquishes. Three savings-banks or were there more? How quickly one's own sisters can go away. *(Again changed, calmly.)* DEAR JOSEPHA. I HOPE THAT YOU ALSO GOT HOME ALL RIGHT, THAT THE STREAKED SKY BEHIND YOU DIDN'T ASTONISH YOU, THAT YOUR TEA WAS STILL THERE, FROM CEYLON. AND THE CRACKERS ON THE DRESSER, FROM YOUR TENTH YEAR. FROM THE MOTHER-LAND. WHICH YOU NEVER OPENED. That's it, I'll write that, I'll have to say that to her. THAT YOUR LAMP WAS ON OR OFF, THAT YOU TWO WERE STILL COMFORTABLE, YOU AND ANNA. THAT YOU MET HER PROPERLY WITH HER FRIENDLY PLAITS. AND THAT YOU SUCCEED IN PRODUCING AGAIN THE SEA, JOSEPHA. For my Samson is coming nearer. And Anna is correct. Without the sea next to him he doesn't look pleasant. Too big. *(She clicks with her tongue.)* With these stripes on his back which you thought so pretty. Old memories, perhaps they should become red cabbage. But they became swords. Violet was always your favorite color, I'll leave them to you, I won't write all that. Only the sea, the sea must appear again. Then he may come nearer, then he may keep what he has, clanking nonsense, his strong shoulders. COME BACK. COME BACK it goes. YOUR SISTER. YOUR SISTER. If it goes COME BACK. *(After a pause.)* But I think it does.

ANNA and
JOSEPHA *(from nowhere, as if they were reciting a poem)*:
    We will be right in the end
    It will come back again

ANNA: Return.

JOSEPHA: Come back.

ANNA and
JOSEPHA: It will come back again: the sea
    with all the eggs that lay hidden in it.

ANNA *(shyly)*: Concealed.

JOSEPHA: Hidden.

ANNA and
JOSEPHA: With all the eggs which lay hidden in it,
    the green ones and the bright ones,
    those blown out, that swim above
    and the others,
    with the edible ones, thin-coated,
    those trod on by the short-tailed eel,
    with the deep-sea blackbirds —

ANNA: Fish-hooks.

ANNA and
JOSEPHA: With the deep-sea blackbirds, fish-hooks,
     short of breath, oblong, dead or alive.

JOSEPHA: Hand me another Dutch biscuit, Anna.

ANNA: With the shells and pieces of shells.

JOSEPHA *(chewing)*: Just a moment.

ANNA: Should I clear away the views from the motherland?

JOSEPHA: No.

ANNA: Put out the light?

JOSEPHA: Leave it.

In the open air.

ROSALIE *(anxiously)*: That is correct.

From nowhere.

ANNA: Are you finished now?

JOSEPHA: Now.

ANNA and
JOSEPHA: With the shells and pieces of shells,
     the oblong virgins, ingots of iron.

In the open air.

ROSALIE: My dear sisters.

From nowhere.

ANNA and
JOSEPHA: Recorded ocean panthers, ocean jaguars,
     Ocean and shelter stands, serenades.

JOSEPHA: Lala.

ANNA: Josepha!

ANNA and
JOSEPHA: Ocean panthers, ocean jaguars.
     When we say RETURN AGAIN.

JOSEPHA: COME —

ANNA: Not yet.

ANNA and
JOSEPHA: When we say —

ANNA *(quickly)*: COME BACK AGAIN!

JOSEPHA: It's COME!

ANNA: No, just wait Josepha!

JOSEPHA: When we say —
     What's the matter, Anna?

ANNA: I would like another piece of tea cake.

JOSEPHA: There are only biscuits left, the Dutch ones.

ANNA: Then give me one *(Chewing.)* Hard, dry.

JOSEPHA: That doesn't sound like you.

ANNA: Exchanged, already in the cradle. Do you have more tea?

JOSEPHA: Exchanged, already beside the shrubs.

ANNA: That sounds like you, Josepha.

In the open air.

ROSALIE: That sounds like you. Even if you remain and are —

From nowhere.

ANNA *(sobbing)*: That sounds like you.

JOSEPHA: Seriously, it is all gone. We must go over to the salt.

In the open air.

ROSALIE: Our dear sister. *(Desperately.)* Josepha, Josepha. What did I do? A March plant, a whim, closed the door to the pikes, to the blind-worm, to the negligently stretched ropes. With a name-day, rights and duties. Rights and duties. And Anna who wasn't supposed to be more than a hurried hymn, a kind of conclusion, a greeting blessing, a winter cloud etcetera. Well what am I? One of these fabricators, one of those nest-robbers, who are not satisfied to bring Anna to Anna, Josepha to Josepha?

From nowhere.

ANNA and
JOSEPHA: We will be right in the end.
       We the superfluous ambassadors,
       Members of an artifical Navy,
       unburnt, unshorn.
       We, the collectors and market-goers,
       unamused by the burst guts
       of lower species,
       we, the insignificant outbuildings
       for the kindergartens of the sectarians,
       rosettes, sections, mortar strokes,
       we small people who have been saved, who
       sought the end in the shell mountain, but no nuts.

ANNA *(shocked)*: Oh I see!

ANNA and
JOSEPHA: We temple facades out of air,
       we named and unnamed partners in conversation,
       we dissolved bus stops,
       unexamined parts of the second John Donne edition
       and so forth. We fabricated sisters —

ANNA: Discovered, discovered! That's what it is isn't it, Josepha? That's what it was, wasn't it? When the Hercules landed, they forgot us for a minute, but then they found us, in tears squeezed

138

behind a cabin door to the relief of everyone. Uncle Solomon was with us even if he left and went back, he took us by the arm while our parents hurried before us, our mother with her hat veil, over the hot sand in search of a car. Isn't that the way it was Josepha?

JOSEPHA: That's not the way it was.

ANNA: But how then, how was it? Did the boat go? Was its name Hercules? Did someone get lost and then found again? Who? One ought to know that. It would really depend on it!

JOSEPHA *(murmuring)*: Bus stops,
unexamined parts of the second John Donne edition —

ANNA *(impatiently)*: And so forth.

JOSEPHA: Now I have lost the thread.

ANNA: We sisters of fiction.

JOSEPHA: We sisters of fiction,
if we tell —
Tell — tell,
if we tell —

In the open air.

ROSALIE: Wait Samson!

From nowhere.

JOSEPHA: Can you help me Anna?

ANNA: That you say I should have told you what I didn't want to tell?

In the open air.

ROSALIE: It will be over soon. Leave the strip of sand between us. I should say: Between us many. For your people have increased. Can you decline GOOSE or FOREST FOWL? GANDER? Then just try it. Only the — let's say the third cases. Honest. What are three birds? I could make it much harder for you.

From nowhere.

JOSEPHA: I have forgotten how it goes but you know Anna.

ANNA *(calmly)*: I'll try to remember.

JOSEPHA: Should we recite it again?

ANNA *(exasperated)*: Once more without me discovering who was there first. Who made up the story of Uncle Solomon? About the unaccustomed sand, the parents hurrying ahead, the fire? Or who retold the story and based on what. Readers are good sources but there are too many. Remember our Uncle Jacob had a collection of old readers, classified, numbered. But he was

139

probably never born. What do you do with such readers?

JOSEPHA: Listen, Anna.

ANNA: And I would also like to know the number of the cabin door which jammed during the trip and behind which we were hidden, this arrival in general. The ship was spacious I know you want to say it. Already during the trip our parents got lost often. I remember that was told to us. And it is possible that we had been hidden behind a false cabin door. 619 maybe instead of 693. But I would like to know the number, Josepha, even if it were two or even more numbers. I have this tendency towards exactness. *(When Josepha doesn't answer.)* The crossing was calm wasn't it? Only in the fifth night did it begin to rain, and it rained the entire night. Except from three to four.

JOSEPHA *(impatiently)*: Yes, yes.

ANNA: Our mother took cologne water, diluted, and went to the ship's barber.

JOSEPHA: I don't recognise you any more.

In the open air.

ROSALIE: It will be finished soon Samson. You already have the goose right. Now the forest fowl. No not the gander, the forest fowl lay between them. And leave your giraffe in peace, it already looks enough like you. You must move more carefully with these swords on your back.

From nowhere.

JOSEPHA: But if you know what you will never find out, Anna, except perhaps the numbers of the cabin doors, wouldn't it be better then if we began again so that we come in again?

In the open air.

ROSALIE: Good, Samson, now the most difficult part. The gander, plural, third case!

From nowhere.

JOSEPHA: From the end. It will be enough.

ANNA *(quietly)*: Temple facades made of air

JOSEPHA *(eagerly)*: We named and unnamed conversation partners, dissolved bus stops

ANNA and
JOSEPHA: Unexamined parts of a second John Donne edition and so forth. We will be right in the end, we sisters of fiction —

JOSEPHA: If we say —

ANNA: COME BACK.

JOSEPHA: COME BACK. That's it. That's it, Anna.

ANNA: If we say

ANNA and
JOSEPHA: COME BACK!

In the open air, roaring.

ROSALIE: What? I don't understand you now. No, false, false. But you no longer have to find the third case. To, for, with, no ganders. The sea has come back. And my sisters, my sisters —

The clanking of Samson's swords.

They are gone, Samson.

ACKNOWLEDGEMENTS

The selections in this edition were originally published in German by S. Fischer Verlag as follows:

From: ELIZA ELIZA
Eliza Eliza
Fünf Vorschläge
Mein grüner Esel
Die Puppe
© S. Fischer Verlag, Frankfurt am Main 1965

From: SCHLECHTE WÖRTER
Schlechte Wörter
Wisconsin und Apfelreis
Dover
Der Gast
© S. Fischer Verlag GmbH, Frankfurt am Main 1976

From: ZU KEINER STUNDE
Französische Botschaft
Tauben und Wölfe
© S. Fischer Verlag, Frankfurt am Main 1957

From: AUCKLAND
Die Schwestern Jouet
© S. Fischer Verlag GmbH, Frankfurt am Main 1969

From: WO ICH WOHNE
Weisse Chrysanthemen
© 1954, 1957, 1961, 1963 S. Fischer Verlag, Frankfurt am Main

From: VERSCHENKTER RAT
Zuspruch an einen Mann
Neuer Bund
In welchen Namen
Teil der Frage
Selbstgebaut
Übermorgen
Zeitlicher Rat
Mein Vater
Gebirgsrand
Tagsüber
Breitbrunn
Widmung
Restlos
Schneeleute
Einunddreissig
Dreizehn Jahre
Möglichkeiten
Marianne
Meiner Grossmutter
Unsere Frau
Alter Blick
Chinesischer Abschied
Briefwechsel
Abgezählt
© S. Fischer Verlag GmbH, Frankfurt am Main 1978

ILSE AICHINGER

Ilse Aichinger was born on November 1, 1921, in Vienna. She spent her early childhood near Linz before returning to Vienna to receive her secondary education. The Anschluss of March, 1938, effected Aichinger directly, for her mother—with whom she remained after the divorce of her parents—was Jewish. While Aichinger's twin sister escaped to England, she herself remained in Austria and saw many of her relatives and friends deported to concentration camps. After the war, in 1945, she began studies of medicine, but after two years left these and became a reader for S. Fischer Verlag, the publishing house which published her first work, *Die grössere Hoffnung*, in 1948. This novel was later published in English translation by Atheneum in New York under the title *Herod's Children*. In the early 1950s Aichinger collaborated in the founding of the Academy for Design in Ulm/Württemberg. She was married in 1953 to the esteemed poet Günter Eich, now deceased. The couple lived in various Bavarian villages before they moved to Grossgmain near Salzburg, where Aichinger continues to live with her mother. Among Aichinger's many literary honors are the Group 47 Prize (1952), the Bremen Prize for Literature (1955), and the Austrian State Prize for Literature (1975).

Library of Congress Cataloging in Publication Data

Aichinger, Ilse.
    Selected poetry & prose.

    I. Title. II. Title: Selected poetry and prose.
PT2601.I26A23 1983   833'.914   83-14867
ISBN 0-937406-25-2
ISBN 0-937406-26-0 (ltd.)
ISBN 0-937406-24-4 (pbk.)